LIFE'S COMPLINE

A Journey Just Begun

BETTY CREAMER

CONTENTS

Acknowledgments

A book such as this does not emerge from one individual person but grows as a living document imagined, birthed, and community-nurtured.

Six years ago when I retired (defined as continuing some degree of work but without a salary), I explored the idea of continued theological education at Bloy House (The Episcopal Theological School of Los Angeles). The most gracious Dean and President, the Very Rev. Sylvia Sweeney, Ph. D. welcomed me into a community of learning, growth, and adventure.

The Holy Spirit enlivens the fertile grounds of the weekend program classrooms, chapel, and community to regularly set my soul aflame. This book emerged from Dean Sweeney's Pastoral Liturgics class, and I thank her and my fellow students for the discussions and encouragement which brought thoughts and dreams into outward and visible practices and writings. I also thank the Rev. Dr. Sheryl Kujawa-Holbrook for reviewing the initial ideas and writing plus providing me with additional reference materials. Dr. Jim Dunkley, Bloy House Chaplain and Professor, who also lives in a senior community, engaged with me and others in conversation about pastoral needs of such communities over Bloy House Friday night dinners and Saturday lunches. Thank you, Jim.

With deepest gratitude, I thank the Grace & Peace Chapel portion of the priesthood of all believers for their lives and ministry as they join up with God's mission in our neighborhood. These people embraced the domestic church/monastic practices described in this book and continue to live these practices themselves while serving as Senior Evangelists and sharing their experiences with others.

With thanksgiving for over fifty years of faithful friendship which now extends into our Compline Years:

Bonnie, Chris, and Jamie—friends in laughter, friends in tears, friends in faith.

"Ever shall we stand together, Winthrop daughters, side by side."—*Alma Mater*

A Word in Time of Pandemic:

I completed the body of this book in February, 2020 with a vision of congregations and individuals using the book as a tool for developing domestic church/monastic practices which support all people but especially the elderly in living out Baptismal vows as part of the priesthood of believers for all of life. In my limited world view and vision at that time, I had a vision of these practices just as I stated in this book— i.e., practices begun in the community of faith and continuing even when a person could no longer be part of the physical community gathered for corporate worship.

That vision continues, but how the vison and practice expanded suddenly within days of the completion of my writing. Enter COVID-19. When the coronavirus hit our world, we gathered on one Sunday when we placed our circle of chairs further apart and made some adjustments to the way we distributed Holy Communion. By the following Sunday, we moved (at the direction of Bishops) to "Communion in one kind" as we distributed bread only to the congregation.

By the middle of the following week, the guidelines from health and government officials plus bishops resulted in cancellation of services. In our senior resort here in the

California desert, the seasonal residents and visitors who planned to remain through April abruptly packed and departed for their permanent homes. Our Canadian friends raced for the northern border with the fear of closed borders pushing them to make the trip as quickly as possible.

As the Canadians raced for the northern border, year-round residents raced for the supermarkets and emptied shelves of toilet paper, hand-sanitizer, and food staples.

Soon we found ourselves in the midst of weeks of "shelter-in-place" edicts, massive job losses, stunning numbers of deaths and severe illness, and hurried adjustments in all aspects of what once had been "normal" life.

The domestic church/monastic practices our local community of faith developed and deployed over the previous two years for daily use but with special intention as spiritual practices for times when a person could not be physically present in the gathered community of faith suddenly became intensely vital to each of us.

During the virus outbreak, the media reported a surge in the legal business regarding wills. While those reports dealt specifically with wills as the legal matters regarding one's assets and heirs after one's death, I imagine that many people also prepared or reviewed "advanced directive" documents in terms of what the person desired as end-of-life care.

Thinking of those medical directives led me to make the suggestion that as readers progress through this book, they might engage in some thoughts (and ideally some writing) concerning spiritual advanced directives. That is, what you want as spiritual care and ministry if/when your physical (and perhaps, mental) condition results in loss of independence including your usual active presence in the worshipping community.

I offer these suggestions as a starting point for preparation of such a spiritual advanced directive:

1. In what ways do you envision continuing belonging, belief, and behavior?
2. How do you wish to maintain connection with your congregation?
3. What resources do you wish for your congregation to provide for you (i.e., devotional materials such as *Forward Day by Day*, the Advent and Lenten study materials, Sunday bulletins and readings)?
4. What spiritual gifts do you wish to use to continue to join up with God's mission in the neighborhood in your new setting?
5. What support from the community of faith enables your continued ministry?

6. What current spiritual practices you use do you wish to continue throughout all your life?
7. What assistance from others might you need in order to continue those practices?
8. What practices in this book might you use or adapt for your continued use?

--Betty Creamer, Holy Week, 2020

Even in old age they will still produce fruit;

They will remain vital and green.

–Psalm 92:14 NRSV

THE COMPLINE YEARS

There was also a prophet, Anna the daughter of Phanuel, of the tribe of Asher. She was of a great age, having lived with her husband seven years after her marriage, then as a widow to the age of eighty-four. She never left the temple but worshiped there with fasting and prayer night and day. At that moment she came and began to praise God and to speak about the child to all who were looking for the redemption of Jerusalem.

–Luke 2:36-38 NRSV

I hadn't thought about those ladies in almost fifty years. Preparing for All Saints Day recently, I pondered the idea of the "great cloud of witnesses" and, more specifically, my gratitude for those I know to be surrounding me. As my memory scrolled through the years, I came to a long-forgotten piece of my life.

I grew up in a large church which had a Youth Sunday tradition. On a Sunday in the spring, the teens took over the leadership positions in the church—including serving as "teacher" for Sunday School classes. In the spring of my junior year of high school, I received the Youth Sunday assignment as teacher for the T.E.L. class. For the uninitiated in the rites of naming Sunday School classes, "The Eldest Ladies", those over age 70 made up this class. Youth Sunday passed in the usual way, school ended for the year, and sometime in the latter days of that last summer of my high school years, one of the ladies in the T.E.L. class approached me at church and told me that the ladies wanted me to serve as their Sunday School teacher when the new year began in September.

Why? Such a thing had not been done before, and I have no knowledge of any continuation of such a practice. Did these ladies get together and say, "Why don't we ask that nice Creamer kid to be our Sunday School teacher; so someday when she's a priest, she will talk about us on All Saints' Sunday?"

Definitely not that!! Maybe no one else wanted the job—though they certainly could have gathered for a discussion of the lessons from the curriculum without having a formal "teacher". My only conviction concerning the process comes from my belief in how the Holy Spirit works. Mystery, Mystery, Holy Mystery.

Who were these women? I remember a small classroom with perhaps a dozen women. When the Sunday School year began in the fall of my senior year of high school (1968), these women were all over 70 years old; so they would all have been born in the 1800's! Most, if not all, were widows. They had lived through two world wars, the Korean War, and some had great-grandsons fighting in Vietnam. They had lived through the Great Depression, planted Victory Gardens, raised families, and known illnesses and deaths in their own families.

They came to church in clean, pressed, cotton dresses in spring and summer or scratchy wool skirts and jackets in the winter and carried well-worn Bibles which contained the language of a seventeenth century king and bard—a Bible in which the Holy Spirit was just a Ghost of who I now know Her to be.

I don't remember their names even though I surely know the family names, but I remember their peace. They radiated a strength of faith and a peace based on that faith.

They prayed for me. I know they did even though we never discussed praying for each other. I never spoke to them about the events and concerns of my teen life and certainly never asked them to pray for me as I took the SAT, applied to college, or had state championship competitions in the next week. I know that I read my Bible each day and prayed during those days; and I remember praying for my boyfriend but have no memory of praying for the T.E.L. ladies. Well, perhaps the boyfriend was the more important person in my life at that point!! Still, I know they prayed for me; and I know they surround me today as part of the great cloud of witnesses.

I wonder—did they have to get someone's permission to name me as their Sunday School teacher? We had a superintendent of Sunday School who had the responsibility to secure teachers. However, he was probably a family member of at least one of the ladies. While men held the leadership positions in the church, these ladies formed a most formidable matriarchy; so I have no doubt who won any argument. However, the drive to church during my senior year always included some muttering from my mother about the inappropriateness of having a teenager as Sunday School teacher for adults!

Back to the original question: Why? Holy Spirit, yes, definitely; but I wish I could ask these ladies and know a more concrete answer. Now that I approach the age of these ladies, I think that perhaps these ladies saw something of the Holy Spirit working in this teen. Perhaps they had a calling even then to surround this teen with their prayers as part of their lives then and as part of their lives in the world to come. Perhaps they longed for a way to continue their ministry and contributions to the life of the Church long after younger women had taken their former roles in leadership. Maybe, they wanted someone in the church to SEE them.

Now, half a century later, we no longer have a T.E.L. Sunday School class, but we have a T.E.L. (and M.) church! The women and men of what I have come to think of as the Compline Years (ages 65 and older) comprise a large and increasing percentage of church members. Current statistics show that the median age for an Episcopalian is 56 with 35% of church members aged 65 and older plus another 31% ages 50-64. (1)

A 2014 Survey of Episcopal Congregations revealed:

> A large majority (73%) of Episcopal congregations report that more than half of their members are age 50+. Twenty-seven percent of Episcopal congregations report that more than half of their members are age 65 or older. (2)

The baby-boomers of today project a far different picture of aging than did those dear ladies in the church during my teen years. We hear phrases such as "seventy is the new forty" to indicate the fact that seniors continue to be active and productive well past retirement.

As the Baby Boomers began to enter the Compline years, several commercial enterprises sought (quite successfully) to accommodate the needs and desires of this generation. An entire industry of "55 and better" housing and resorts emerged; universities as well as churches and other religious organizations opened "active senior" housing communities; and the Recreational Vehicle industry now reports more than 9 million such vehicles in use in the United States.

Many elders have sold the family home and moved to communities away from family; and some choose to travel all or part of the year via RV.

Leisure World (now named Laguna Woods) in Southern California and in Arizona created entire cities of senior housing with a wide range of amenities and activities for active seniors. In the "55 and better" resort where I live in the southern California desert, residents enjoy golf, tennis, pickleball (the fastest growing sport in the U.S.), hot springs spas and pools, and a host of other activities including book clubs, cards, art, quilting, journaling, and more.

While many senior adults do engage in the life-styles described above, statistics show that 10% of people over 65 in the U.S. live in poverty. The National Council on Aging reports that

> over 25 million Americans aged 60+ are economically insecure—living at or below 250% of the federal poverty level ($29,425 per year for a single person). These older adults struggle with rising housing and health care bills, inadequate nutrition, lack of access to transportation, diminished savings, and job loss. (3)

In the "55 and better" community where I live, many of our residents supplement Social Security income by working in the community—odd jobs, house cleaning, pet sitting, meal preparation, and caring for the homes of seasonal residents during the "off season".

Many of the people in the 70+ age group worked when wages were lower and before our current system of retirement savings programs. They spent their working lives in the trust that Social Security would be sufficient for retirement income. Those who receive the Social Security minimum payment at this time receive total monthly income of just under $1000.

Our senior adult church members may include a full range from the financially secure to those living with the reality of fiscal insecurity. Our church members may also display a range of spiritual maturity from those who have been in church from nine months before birth to those who come seeking a place to be less alone plus strength and comfort during the last years of life.

This book addresses pastoral needs of this large group of senior adults living in the Compline Years and advocates for use of ritual practices of domestic church/monasticism to develop and sustain faith practices for life. Part II of this book provides an account of one congregation's journey in development and practice of domestic church/monasticism.

Pastoral Needs

I vow to promote the well-being of all elderly people, doing what I can to honor and respect both aging and the aged and seeing in the old a repository of wisdom and honorable society.

–Rabbi M. Shapiro

"We need more young families in church." "We need a rector who will bring in young people." How often do we hear such statements from church members? After we remind everyone of the priesthood of all believers and that church growth/leadership/outreach belongs to all and not just those ordained, perhaps we will then move forward to develop an active, vibrant ministry with those who currently make up our congregations—including this huge percentage of people in (and approaching) the Compline Years.

I use the term "Compline Years" because the order of Compline in the Daily Office provides prayers at the end of the day, and the Compline years provide seniors with time for prayerful reflection in the latter days of life. While the Compline prayers embrace the hope and faith that the faithful sleep and then awaken to a new day, the Compline of life embodies and animates the hope and faith of the deep sleep of death as part of the journey just begun in the light and love of God in eternity.

This hope, faith, and time of prayerful reflection also involves full, active participation in continuing to live out Baptismal vows.

If we listen to conversations about pastoral needs of the elderly perhaps at a vestry meeting, a church conference, or a seminary classroom, we might find the conversations revolving around pastoral care for shut-ins, the sick, the dying. Yes, we need that care; but beyond those areas of pastoral care, "Christian churches have not on the whole promoted healthy perspectives and futures for older adults." (4)

Older adults need ways to continue to live out Baptismal vows and ways to continue "belonging, belief, behavior" for life and ways to remain connected to the community of faith when they no longer can be physically present in the worshipping community.

Thornton Wilder's drama, "The Long Christmas Dinner" (5) depicts ninety years of Christmas dinners in the life of the Bayard family. A typical production requires a minimalist set which includes a stage left portal hung with colorful fabric. Entry via this portal signifies the birth of a family member. Meanwhile, at the dinner table in the center of the stage, characters add a shawl or a white-haired wig as a symbol of aging. A character's exit via a black curtain on stage right symbolizes the character's death.

Wilder's drama parallels some of the essential themes in our lives as Christians. Baptism, the sacrament of belonging, makes us part of God's family. Rabbi Naomi Levy, writing in Einstein and the Rabbi, provides a dramatic picture of our belonging to God:

> Most of us wear or drive or carry things with designer labels on them. We are walking billboards for the companies that make our clothing, our shoes, our purses, our cars. As if they say something about who we are, I want

you to know that there is a designer label on you right now. And, trust me, it doesn't say Prada or Porsche. It is written across your forehead and across your heart in big capital letters: GOD.

The Creator's seal is on you. Let it inform your actions, your thoughts. God's seal is on you, in your essence. You were created to be a walking advertisement for the One who designed you. (6)

At our baptisms, we become full members of the household of God. Like the members of the Bayard family, we belong at the table. We then take our place at God's table—a table that extends throughout, not just our temporal lives, but ages past and through all eternity.

In Wilder's depiction of the long, celebratory meal, people age. Change happens—a character's move to a wheelchair signifies a loss of ability but not loss of the place at the table. In the aging process, the members of the Bayard family continue to belong at the table, to act and speak in full confidence (belief) as members of the family, and to exhibit behavior consistent with that belonging and belief.

Seniors need an assurance of unconditional love and closeness to God (and to the community of faith as an outward and visible symbol of God's love) at a time when physical and/or mental decline brings fears and insecurities.

For many years, we commonly used belief, belonging, behavior as the sequence for how people came into the church and entered a life of faith. However, in more recent years, we have observed and come to a different sequence—belonging, belief, behavior.

As people age, life events bring the need for belonging into sharper and sharper focus. One cannot enter the Compline Years without having experienced loss in terms of the deaths of family and friends as well as loss, at least in part, due to distance and loss of ability to travel. Statistics show that "over one-fourth (26 percent) of women ages 65-74 lived alone in 2018. This share jumped to 39 percent among women ages 75-84, and to 55 percent among women aged 85 and older." (7)

Furthermore, "More older adults are divorced compared with previous generations. The share of divorced women ages 65 and older increased from three percent in 1980 to 14 percent in 2018, and for men from four percent to 11 percent during the same period." (8)

A lady in her early 70's spoke to me about her own situation. Her husband, ten years older than she, had begun to experience significant and increasing health problems. She spoke of how their social life had revolved around couples in his professional circle, but many of them had died.

She said, "I realize I am going to be alone, and I need to make some friends."

Our resort-based congregation frequently welcomes new people (most often women) who join us for worship and then share the same basic story (with some individualized, specific details). That is, the person's spouse or partner died in the last year or so; and this person has returned to the resort where the couple had lived or visited in previous years. The story usually involves a statement like this: "Our friends 'back home' have died, and the children (if any) have moved away. I am alone, but I know people here are friendly."

Not only do we emphasize belonging at our Eucharistic table, but we have lunch after our Sunday service; and people linger to share food and to have moments of continued belonging. Indeed, our Sunday lunches grew out of observations of how people often lingered an hour or more over a cookie and coffee. Those observations also included listening to conversation during that time, and we learned that people came looking for companionship and support.

The conversations involved sharing stories of loss and grief—usually the death of a spouse. Many of the stories also included heart-rending stories of estrangement from family members. People share their stories, their hurts, and their fears. Coffee hour became a lunch time; and the shared stories led to supportive friendships, discussions of faith, sharing prayer concerns, and plans for social interactions.

Lunch includes the sharing of left-over food, and people take home food not just for the nourishment of another meal but also a time of remembering the belonging at the Eucharistic and luncheon tables and in the community of faith.

The term, Senior Evangelist, comes later in this book with a more expansive discussion; but one of the actions of our Senior Evangelists involves observing the needs of friends and neighbors not in church who might need a meal during a time of illness or to help deal with loneliness. Those observations lead to the packaging of plates of food to distribute to neighbors as we go out into our neighborhoods.

The years after retirement should not represent a retirement FROM work/activities of value but retirement TO a continued, valued vocation. After careful, intense scrutiny and research concerning the promises we make at Baptism, I continually fail to find the liturgy of retirement/release from those vows. Rather, in direct opposition to the idea of such a release, I find every indication that the vows we make at Baptism and reaffirm throughout the Liturgical Year not only endure but allow for continued growth and service.

Recognizing the need for continued belonging and acknowledging the gifts and vocation of seniors enables churches to embrace the riches of the priesthood of all believers—of all ages.

> The inability to speak meaningfully about the
> calling of older adults comes, in part, from a

too-easy collapse of the notion of divine calling with work or career. This collapse seems to situate older adulthood beyond the boundaries of vocation, placing people of advanced years in a life space that somehow seems "finished with vocation" because they are not "productive" or contributing in ways typically recognized as love and service. (9)

Our North American society emphasizes the value of youth via media, advertising, and the vast array of products designed to delay or utterly defeat the aging process. Society (and, to some extent, the medical community) treats death as a defeat. Do we not hear or say that a person "lost his/her battle with cancer/other medical diagnosis"? How do our communities of faith enable the elderly to embrace faith and community and continue to grow spiritually in such a climate? We engage in mutual ministry which continues belonging, belief, and behavior for all of mortal life. This book explores the use of domestic church/monastic practices as a way to aid in that ministry.

The aging process generates physical and cognitive changes with accompanying psychological/spiritual needs. "For most of the elderly in the US, religion has a major role in their life, with about half attending religious services at least weekly." (10). While the psychological/spiritual needs do not fall perfectly into the categories of "belonging, belief, and behavior", those elements provide a framework for exploring and responding to the spiritual needs of the elderly.

Many of our elderly church members claim a lifetime, or at least many years, of belonging to the Church. As members age, they experience situations which remove them from some or all of the worship and activities of the church.

> Acute or chronic physical illness often arouses fears and insecurities, forcing the elder to confront existential issues that previously could be avoided. The disruption of routine caused by illness and hospitalization can upset that internal sense of continuity needed to maintain emotional equilibrium. The elder's sense of self-esteem may be assaulted by their changing physical condition, increasing dependency, loss of control, and sometimes humiliating diagnostic or therapeutic procedures. The need for unconditional love and a feeling of closeness to God may intensity at this time. They need to be able to continue to love and give to others, in spite of limiting circumstances. Physically ill elders need an opportunity to nurture their relationship with God through prayer, scripture, and worship. They need not only to prepare for death, but also for the life they have left. (6)

Elderly church members need ways to remain connected to the community of faith when they cannot be physically present. Diana Butler Bass quotes Barbara Brown Taylor who writes: "In this universe, there is no such thing as an individual apart from his or her relationships." (12) and Archbishop Desmond Tutu who states: "The first law of our being is that we are set in a delicate network of interdependence with our fellow human beings and with the rest of God's creation." (13)

Church members develop strong bonds with each other as they meet at God's table, pray together, and enjoy the social aspects of the faith community (i.e., coffee hour, Advent and Lenten studies, meals together). The individuals whose circumstances prohibit being with their spiritual family experience a heightened sense of loss.

> Narayanasamy (1991) writes regarding spiritual needs of older adults which include "The need to give and receive love; the need to be understood; the need to be valued as a human being; the need for forgiveness, hope and trust; the need to explore beliefs and values; the need to express feelings honestly; the need to express faith or belief; the need to find meaning and purpose in life." (14)

The need for belonging not only continues but grows stronger and more important during the changes and losses experienced in the aging process. Sister Joan Chittister observes: "Whole villages of older women and men have sprung up, segregated from the larger population around them. . . . In a mobile society, families are spread across the country. No one is just dropping in to see grandma anymore." (16)

Elderly Christians seek ways to continue their belonging and participation in their faith community. Indeed, "Religion and Spirituality in the Elderly" finds that

> the elderly's level of religious participation is greater than that in any other age group. For the elderly the religious community is the largest source of social support outside of the family, and involvement in religious organizations is the most common type of voluntary social activity—more common than all other forms of voluntary social activity combined. (17)

Therefore, the need for belonging intensifies as one ages, and this need necessitates pastoral care, attention, and action for ways to maintain that belonging.

While lamenting the many painful realities of aging and holding grief and losses in our hearts, domestic church-monastic practices engage the elderly in developing a sustaining practice for continuing in the life of belonging, belief, and behavior.

Life in our congregations often follows Wilder's drama in which a stage right exit signifies a character's death. Someone else now occupies that character's place at the table.

How often do we hear someone remark during coffee hour that Horace, a 90-year-old recent widower, wasn't here today. Then comes a response: "His daughter came to visit this week and took him to live with her." Or someone announces that Kay, a widow over age 80 who lived alone, broke her hip this week, so her granddaughter came and took her to live with the granddaughter in Seattle. Not death announcements, but "exit, stage right", just the same.

In another version of the departure realities, a person might become homebound or move to a care facility. In these latter situations, the persons may be in our geographical area where people can visit more easily; but they are no longer able to be a part of the community for worship and fellowship.

How do we enable our elderly church members to continue a sense of belonging even when we cannot be together physically? The domestic church/monastic model presented here may be used and adapted in many ways to help meet the need for continued belonging.

Developing domestic church/monastic practices begins with the firm knowledge that each of us belongs to God—now and forever. In these practices, we develop shared rituals and use shared symbols. When elders must leave home and home church, they depart with the shared symbols and rituals and the knowledge that they carry on these practices in continued community with the friends they leave behind. These outward and visible symbols may also have the effect of influencing others around them.

In the Compline years, the elderly experience a decline in physical ability and strength. In addition, these years often require the elderly to give up experiences and possessions. One may no longer be able to drive or to travel; one may need to give up the family home. The loss of autonomy looms large in these years when the losses often come without one's consent, and others may make the decisions about so much of a person's life. In the midst of this intense season of demise, the elderly need more than ever to embrace familiar, sustaining belief in God.

Our liturgies include a confession of faith beginning with the words "I believe" or "We believe". Perhaps in the Compline Years, the elderly may find that some alternate translations of the Latin *credo* provide additional strength. Elders may find additional strength from the creeds by remembering those first words also mean "I trust" or "I depend upon" these tenets of faith. When one can no longer trust or depend upon one's own physical (and, in many cases, mental) abilities, long held and ever-growing spiritual beliefs and practices give the elder strength for this part of the journey.

During these latter years of earthly life, a person usually spends some time determining what is important and why. In our Western culture filled with large homes and many possessions, we often hear people in the senior years speaking of "down-sizing". Couples no longer need the family home once filled with growing children. A widow or widower finds the long-shared dwelling difficult both physically and emotionally. Older singles also seek smaller living spaces requiring less upkeep and expenses.

Others must "down-size" because circumstances (physical, medical, financial) require a move to assisted living or to live with a family member.

Whatever the situation, the process of "down-sizing" requires giving up possessions. One must decide what items remain essential to life (some clothing, toothbrush) and what items support and enhance life (sentimental items).

The elderly may move to a new location in the same community (and remain part of the "home" church), to an assisted living community, to a room in a relative's home, to an "active senior community", or even to a life of full-time recreational vehicle residence and travel. Whatever the circumstances leading to "down-sizing" and the nature of the new living situation, the remaining possessions become even more precious as the outward and visible symbols of the best memories of a long life.

Elders who have lived a life of faith take their beliefs into these years and into new physical spaces. Belief becomes even more important as the elder learns to rest in God's peace and to continue to grow spiritually.

The team of writers in the volume, <u>Reflections on Aging and Spiritual Growth</u> states: "Then there comes the time to let all the talk and thought and everything else go, and just rest with our Friend, our God—just be with the God who dwells within." (18)

The Church has both an enormous opportunity and responsibility to prepare people to enter and navigate the Compline Years with great strength of faith and practices to support continued belief and spiritual growth.

When elders develop and practice domestic church/ monastic rituals in community with those with whom they regularly gather at God's table, they gain strength from the knowledge that others join them in these prayers and practices no matter when or where they engage in the ritual. Thus, they live in the strength of belonging to God and to the spiritual community.

In <u>Aging, Spirituality and Pastoral Care: A Multi-National Perspective</u>, the researchers provide the readers with a term "spiritual thickness" and state:

> In order to confront the questions and challenges of older adulthood, a person must be girded by "thickness" of spiritual resources. In other

words, the transition to older adulthood must first be made in the spiritual dimension. . . . Older adulthood needs a continuing vision of God and God's kingdom and an individual's place in it. (19)

As people move into retirement or a decrease in work hours, some add or increase physical fitness routines. Some Medicare plans include "Silver Sneaker" gym memberships, and senior living facilities often include fitness centers. We see and hear information about vitamins, diet, and exercise in order to gain strength in our muscles and bones. Of course, the earlier in life one gives attention to nutrition and fitness, the better the result.

The same principle holds for faith development. We make and reaffirm our Baptismal promise of faithfulness in "word, prayers, and sacrament", and we need to place emphasis on how to live out this promise. Just as assess to nutritious food and opportunity (and budgeting time) for fitness enables people to live in a healthy body, providing the food and strength training for spiritual growth enables people of all ages to develop the practices necessary for living out this baptismal promise for all of life.

"Many seniors must cope with the loss of a spouse or loved one. Others might be grappling with their own illness or mortality. Faith can provide a support system for handling these tough issues." (20)

While many abilities decline with age, "evidence indicates that for many aging individuals spiritual capacity gradually increases, especially with regards to self-acceptance and perceptions of one's life having integrity." (21)

Universities provide "training tables" for athletes where team members eat meals designed by nutritionists; and those same athletes participate in "strength and conditioning" training to gain the strength and stamina required for athletic performance. We have a "training table" in church, for we come to God's table where we receive the perfect meal to strengthen us for our living into God's mission in our neighborhood.

However, we must give more intention to providing the "strength and conditioning" for our calling from our baptisms until the very end of life on this earth. A runner does not run a marathon on the first day of training. The athlete builds strength for that long run.

Spiritual capacity increases with age, and the elderly (and everyone of all ages) progressively requires the anchor of belief in order to navigate the surging, stormy seas of aging.

> Mature faith involves such a trust and
> dependence on God that it determines how one
> thinks about and acts toward oneself and others
> in daily life. This attitude enables a person to
> transcend negative life events, maintain a sense
> of meaning, hope, and purpose even in the most
> dismal of circumstances, and function on the

highest level (physically, socially, and emotionally) given available resources. Religious faith of this type seldom develops in the absence of hardship or suffering, and it requires the personal experience of having one's faith successfully carry one through a difficult time. . . . While this concept may appear radical to some, it is the key to being able to transcend loss and changes associated with aging. (22)

The elderly person requires opportunities to develop that anchor-place of belief that sustains her/him all the days of life and leads to the joy of knowing that our loving God welcomes us to "strength to strength in the life of perfect service" (23) at the conclusion of this earthly life.

Developing domestic church/monastic practices reinforces and renews faith through ritual. Ritual enables the elderly to recall, remember, and grow faith in this Compline of life. "Bianchi suggests that this period of life 'offers one of the richest periods for growth in meditative interiority.'" (24)

Like the Daily Office, shared domestic church/monastic practices may be observed alone while in the full, strength-filled knowledge that others share the same practices which may include the same structure for prayers, the same readings (i.e. lectionary, *Forward Day by Day),* and have the same physical symbols (i.e. cross, candle) present.

Belief involves both action and memory, and "Participation in ritual can simultaneously move one forward and provide a sense of stability by highlighting continuity. Through the use of ritual emotions can be discharged; identity can be shaped; connections can be developed or restored." (25)

Even when memory fails, elders benefit from rituals connected with faith. David Jackson states that

> to connect with faith and faith in God during spiritual care, prayer (e.g., group prayer, intercessory prayer) has been found to offer a sense of strength and comfort for older people living with dementia. . . Through reading scripture and the Bible (or equivalent), some older people remain connected to their faith and faith in God and are given strength and comfort. (26)

When the effects of aging dictate that an elder must leave home and the home faith community, she/he may sustain faith and sense of community by continuing in the faith community's learned and shared domestic church/monastic practices.

In conversation with a friend from long-ago seminary days, I inquired about my friend's mother. She reported with a pronounced sense of joy that her mother continued her life in a care facility where she, though now totally blind, enjoyed playing the piano for community hymn-sings.

My friend's mother continued her life of faith and continued to serve God and those in her neighborhood long after she had had to give up many of her former activities and much of her independence. While this dear lady could no longer see the faces around her, I have no doubt that she continually saw the face of God within her heart.

Some sports, basketball and football among those, involve four periods of play. While the time in each quarter increases as players progress from the earliest ages through high school, university, and professional play, the four-quarter format remains the same.

In recent years, some teams and fans have added a ritual of raising hands displaying four fingers prior to the final period of play. The meaning of the gesture depends upon a team's current score. The team ahead in the scoring views the gesture as a reminder to take care of business, to keep up their efforts to the end. The ritual gesture's overall meaning for all players and fans represents the goal of giving one's best all the way to the game's end—even if victory might seem hopeless.

One of the worst edicts from media commentators involves the statement indicating that a team obviously has given up and now plays with a "don't care" attitude. In fact, just the opposite, even in a loss, teams and fans want to hear the analysts' words of praise in that players showed tenacious grit and enthusiasm to the very end. Likewise, we celebrate and recognize marathon runners—not only the one who finishes first and perhaps sets a new record for the fastest finish; but we often see a news report featuring the person who finishes last—sometimes even the following day. In this latter report, the runner makes the news because of perseverance and commitment all the way to the end no matter how long and hard the journey. The runner believed that he/she would finish the race and acted on that belief. So, too, seniors act on belief and live their commitment to God no matter how long the journey continues. St. Paul expressed his reflection as his own life moved into the final earthly days: "I have finished the race; I have kept the faith." --II Timothy 4:7, NRSV

Belonging to the family of God via Baptism and living out our faith (belief) informs our behavior throughout life. How we join up with God's mission and the realities of our neighborhood can and will change as we age, but the basis for our behavior as children of God continues to inform how we live.

Financial planners currently remind us that we need to plan for 30 or more years of "retirement". In the "55 and better" community where I live, I regularly see my neighbors over the age of 80 and even 90 engaging in hiking, golf, swimming, tennis, pickleball, waterball (volleyball in the swimming pool) as well as feeding the hungry, tutoring, and other service activities in the larger community.

At the same time, other seniors retreat into a life of bitterness and isolation—using a movie title, they become "grumpy old men" (and women!). We all know some of them—quite different from my seminary friend's mother and so many others we know.

What a delight to hear one of Sunday's lectors read a lesson in such a way that those in the congregation know absolutely that this reader does not simply read words but proclaims God's love and care in a way which reflects a life of walking with God, and one also knows that this lector goes out from the time of corporate worship to actively work to increase the Kingdom of God in the world around her/him.

By empowering all the baptized to truly live as a priesthood of all believers, the Church sends out a mighty spirit into the world. No need to retreat into darkness or become the grumpy, old senior when one, through the grace of God, lives in God's light.

Growing older does bring painful changes—deaths of family members and friends, loss of physical and mental abilities, loss of independence. We acknowledge and lament losses and continue to walk in God's strength.

Morrie tells Mitch that "Aging is not just decay, you know. It's growth. . .it's also the positive that you're going to die, and that you live a better life because of it." (27)

Continuing to engage in the familiar behaviors of Christian life and the community of faith imbues elders with strength, resilience, and peace even when those behaviors take place in a new and different setting.

> Faith involves believing that persons are worthwhile, important, and of value, even if helpless and dependent upon others, because God cares about and values every human being, regardless of their capacity to produce for society. Mature faith involves putting on positive attitudes and/or taking steps toward constructive action despite feelings to the contrary. . . . By reading scripture or other aids to devotion, spending time in personal prayer and meditation, and worshipping within a community of believers, persons nurture their relationship with God . . . . (28)

In our congregations, do we look at the elderly as those "on the way out" or as people vital to the present and continuing living out faith, joining up with God's mission, and moving the present Kingdom of God on earth ever forward?

A significant number of colleges and universities have either constructed near-by retirement residences or formed relationships with such. Residents of those facilities engage in cultural and athletic events as well as academic classes at the near-by schools, and both the retirees and students benefit from the mutual experiences and learning—and sometimes with retirees leading those experiences and sharing lifetimes of knowledge and experience.

In my own experience, auditing a class each semester at a seminary greatly enriches my continued ministry. The weekend seminary program features several "past retirement" professors (including one over age 90) who share a vast wealth of knowledge and experience to a student body varying in age from younger adults to those well into the Compline years. What a joy to engage with those who come to study and learn as a response to the Holy Spirit's leading them into unknown paths of joy, tears, service, and growth.

William Clements paints a word picture of aging and religious roles:

> Religious roles, however, do not have to be relinquished at any age. There is not a retirement age for religious roles. Furthermore, the religious role encompasses more than participation in the church, it includes private and everyday religious behavior, as well as the feeling that religion has meaning. Through nonorganizational or daily religious practices, the religious role is a salient factor in the lives of the elderly. For example, the older person whose church attendance is limited by physical and/or social factors associated with the aging process, may at the same time be highly committed—cognitively, emotionally, and morally—to their church. Their faith may be

strong, their personal decisions may be made in relationship to 'the faith of the church', and their feelings of self-identity with and love and loyalty for the church may remain. (29)

With such commitment to faith and church by the elderly, how does the church respond with a commitment just as strong to the elderly?

Reflection:

One of the severe threats of retirement is the feeling of being worthless now that one is no longer economically or socially productive. This feeling has theological dimensions as well; many elders have felt the threat of abandonment by God once they could no longer be active, especially in church work.

--Arthur H. Becker, <u>Ministry with Older Persons</u>

1. How do you view the idea of "Compline Years" as a description for the latter years of life?

2. How does your congregation prepare and equip people for and enable continued belonging, belief, behavior when a person can no longer be physically present in the worshipping community?

3. As you contemplate your own "Compline Years", how do you wish to continue to live out your Baptismal vows?

4. What preparation and support do you need and want from your congregation for that process?

Prayer: Holy Mother/Father God, thank you for creating us and embracing us as your children through the waters of our Baptism; Holy Redeemer, Jesus, thank you for teaching us how to love, believe, and pray; Holy Spirit, guide and support us all our days as we love and serve God and each other. Amen.

HOLY GROUND

Older adults may call forth in others untested capacities of loyalty, commitment, justice, and love. This too is an important element in the purposes of God. (30)

Now there was a man in Jerusalem whose name was Simeon; this man was righteous and devout, looking forward to the consolation of Israel, and the Holy Spirit rested on him. It had been revealed to him by the Holy Spirit that he would not see death before he had seen the Lord's Messiah. Guided by the Spirit, Simeon came into the temple; and when the parents brought in the child Jesus, to do for him what was customary under the law, Simeon took him in his arms and praised God, saying,
* "Master, now you are dismissing your servant in peace,*
*   according to your word;*
for my eyes have seen your salvation,
which you have prepared in the presence of all peoples,
a light for revelation to the Gentiles
*   and for glory to your people Israel."*

And the child's father and mother were amazed at what was being said about him. Then Simeon blessed them and said to his mother Mary, "This child is destined for the falling and the rising of many in Israel, and to be a sign that will be opposed so that the inner thoughts of many will be revealed—and a sword will pierce your own soul too."
--Luke 2:25-35 NRSV

First, we may begin by viewing our elderly church members as Holy Ground—a foundation of lives of faith and practice providing the church with examples of living, breathing baptismal promises.

However, researchers exploring life-long Christian vocation find that:

> First-person reports from older adults themselves suggest that if today's older adults are on pedestals, those pedestals must be located in broom closets and basements where they are invisible and ignored. The gap between the ideal view of older adults in Christian tradition and the actuality of real peoples' lives in contemporary North America brings into question the credibility of theological claims that older adults continue to experience a calling. Currently, churches and their theologians suffer from a distinct inability to articulate the share of vocation in the waning years of life." (31)

In the church as well as in the world, we far too often equate productivity and human value with career and financial income. When a person in our congregation can no longer walk steadily with a chalice, prepare meals, sing in the choir, prepare the altar, participate in meetings, or organize activities, do we "retire" the person? Viewing our elderly as Holy Ground might well enable the church to continue to honor that fertile soil and give fresh articulation to vocation in senior years.

We then move from a vision of "retirement" to the true vision of vocation for life, a vision centered not around the elder's limitations but around the elder's relationship with God and God's mission in our neighborhood.

> But if vocation is about God's call to persons (and communities) claiming them across the whole of their lives, surely God calls older adults amid all their differences within the time of older adulthood, to vocations of service and love, too. Absent the features that play such a critical role in the preceding years of middle and even late adulthood, we instead find older adult vocation particularly emphasizing who we are as creatures of God, *how* we are in relationship (with God, with others), and *what* capacities we evoke in others, rather than what we produce or accomplish. (32)

Teaching domestic church practices (early and often) provides one way to enable the elderly to continue vital ministry throughout their lives. Engaging the community in development of monastic practices to combine with domestic church provides the church with an avenue for commissioning elderly (and others in the community) to a life of service and leads all members of the community to value and affirm domestic church/monasticism as one way to continue to live faith for all of life.

After all, vocation and our spiritual gifts come from God; and the refreshing breeze and prevailing wind of the Holy Spirit's power does not fail.

Often pastoral care for the elderly consists primarily of providing Holy Communion in homes of those homebound as well as those in hospital or care facilities, and perhaps a regularly scheduled service at a care facility.

What happens in the church congregation when the above ceases to be "what WE do for THEM" and becomes moments of profound grace and mutual ministry (or maybe the balance scale tilts more to the elderly's ministry to, for, and with the community) by engaging in and communicating to the community the profound prayers and witness of those who continue as Holy Ground?

Reflection:

The process of physical diminishment and the struggles we have in this "mortal tent," to quote the apostle Paul, are actually invitations to go deeper with God and to have hope. This involves transforming mortality and anticipating resurrection.

--R. Paul Stevens, <u>Aging Matters</u>

1. How can one's diminishments and struggles result in a deeper faith and hope?

2. How have you known and experienced people whose lives may well be described as "Holy Ground"?

3. What personal spiritual practices and community support enables a person to develop the foundation for living as "Holy Ground"?

Prayer: Holy God, support us all our days as we live as your beloved creatures and children; may our lives continue to enable and support faith in others; and may the power of the Holy Spirit lead us to walk always as children of light and hope. Amen.

A New Heart

I will give you a new heart and put a new spirit in you. I will remove your stony heart from your body and replace it with a living one.

—Ezekiel 36:26 CEB

Someone in our resort community once told me about a neighbor on the heart-transplant list. While the neighbor awaited a physical heart, many enter the Compline Years and our communities searching for a new heart and spirit.

Thankfully, the reality of a new heart and new spirit found in Ezekiel continues to exist. Not only exist, but this new heart and new spirit process requires no waiting, no specific blood type, and no financial qualifications.

Both statistics and anecdotal information demonstrate the varied ways in which people in the Compline Years seek that new heart and new spirit—even if they cannot name what they seek.

In our resort community built around social and healthy activities, not everyone who seeks to assuage loneliness or to achieve better health chooses to engage in activities leading to fulfilling those goals. Such thinking and choices sound puzzling, but people often verbalize their choices. Someone standing by the hot-springs-fed pools and spas says, "I know the hot water would ease my joint pain, but I've never gotten into the water." Some reasons follow the first statement— have not purchased a swimsuit, etc. Others look at the lists of activities spanning from early morning into the evening, sigh, and return home to sit alone in front of the television. Before one judges too harshly, one might think of the times we all say something like: "I know I would feel better if I got some exercise; or ate more fruits and vegetables; or drank more water. Many in our communities also have much deeper longings which they may not be able to articulate so easily. People may easily and often express the need to lose weight or increase exercise; however, expressing the need for a new spiritual heart takes far more contemplation and courage.

Elizabeth MacKinlay, in The Spiritual Dimension of Ageing, addresses the searching which accompanies the elder years:

> From wisdom comes the ability to construct one's individual and final life meaning; the spirit grows, finding meaning in being, accepting the inevitable losses of life, and letting go of things that are no longer important. Meaning making in the later years becomes a critical aspect of effective aging. And it is this search for the final meaning of life which is truly a component of the spiritual dimension. (33)

Some come to our churches looking for this "meaning making", a new heart of faith; however, even more encounter Holy Ground and meet our Senior Evangelists who join up with God's mission in the neighborhood—in whatever form the neighborhood takes. Perhaps we should hang a sign outside our church meeting space and add announcements at community gatherings stating "New Hearts and New Spirits Available NOW and FREE!"? At the same time, we acknowledge and support the mission of our Senior

Evangelists who indeed represent the "first responders" in this new heart of faith journey.

The new heart and new spirit come freely from God but not without a person's mind and heart ready for transformation. At the time when people enter a life free of structured work time and with less structured personal time, the transformation required for the new heart and new spirit requires a new structure for how one uses time, abilities, and money. The new heart and new spirit actually involve a change in vocation—i.e., God's call for how the person lives life as an agent of God's mission in the neighborhood. The new heart calls a person into that vocation of being Holy Ground and living as a Senior Evangelist.

In developing and implementing domestic church and monastic practices, we must include in our own hearts and prayers the "others"—i.e., the sheep outside the fold; those seeking, however unknowingly, a new heart and a new spirit. If 60% of those in the Compline Years regularly attend church, easy math shows that the other 40% do not.

Living in a senior community brings me into relationships with people in ways far different from typical parish or chaplaincy ministry. My neighbors and I see each other on walks, at the swimming pool, lounging in the thermal spas, engaging in resort activities, and making the trip via golf cart to the rubbish compactor.

If I don't see my 91-year-old neighbor on his morning walk and later passing by in his golf cart on his way to play water ball, I check to be sure he is well. If I don't show up for my 8 a.m. swim, neighbors notice and check on me. We live in community and act as caring neighbors and friends.

Sounds great—and is. However, with the good-neighbor life also comes more intimate knowledge of each other and habits good and not-so-good. These realities inform and direct some of my life as a chaplain among these neighbors.

The nature of life in a "55 and better" resort means that "birth" in this community comes at age 55, and everyone arrives here from another geographical place. Many seek the hot water and desert climate for health reasons.

Another reality—we all live in the final quarter of life, and, in some profound way, we have a resort community which also lives as a community of grief. No week goes by without requests for prayers for a personal or family illness (often a diagnosis of impending fast decline and death). Rarely does a day pass in this community of more than 1000 residents during the "high season" (November through April) without a visit from EMS to someone's home. Reports of deaths come frequently, and the community experiences another phase of grief when long-time residents and/or seasonal friends can no longer live independently or make the seasonal trip to their resort homes.

Often people stop me in the pool area, club house, or perhaps while checking the mail or attending an activity to ask for prayers for self or others. The conversation tends to begin with some almost apologetic words such as "I don't go to church" or "I'm not a believer, but . . .". At other times, the person might say, "My husband just received a diagnosis of . . . . We haven't been people of faith, but I'm thinking that I want to know about something beyond where we are now."

Our congregation worships in clubhouse space with lunch following our celebration of Holy Eucharist. Each Sunday, we look around the swimming pool, billiards room, laundry room, library, and other common areas before we eat to invite others to join us. Our lunches have included the lonely, grieving recent widower who one of our Senior Evangelists found sitting outside the laundry room; a recent widow sitting alone at a pool-side table; a young man refinishing floors in the clubhouse; office staff working in the reception area; and three men who were digging a trench for urgent electrical repairs.

Yes, we would very much like to have people be present at the worship service, but we often find lonely people around us who greatly enjoy the time of sitting at table for lunch and conversation. Some of them do indeed become part of the worshipping community, but the hospitality extends to all. We know that belonging comes first!

One of the best evangelists in the community for years has been a Jewish neighbor who actively tells people that the Episcopal community welcomes them and that they will find hospitality and companionship in our community.

We also plan our food in order to have food for anyone who wants to share the left-overs—with the hope and prayer that the food for later assuages some loneliness and brings memory of time together in community and the desire to return again and again to that community. Leftovers also provide meals for those in our neighborhoods who our Senior Evangelists know to be sick, caring for a sick person, or just in need of a symbol of caring.

We have learned in our community that our domestic church/monastic practices and especially the outward and visible symbols of those practices that friends and neighbors see in our homes have brought others into our community of faith.

A former chaplain here became one of my first and closest friends in this community. Before declining health necessitated her move to a location near one of her children (a location and move for which she had planned after the death of her husband), a life-threatening situation resulted in transportation to a local hospital for several weeks of treatment.

On the first Sunday of her hospitalization, I went to the hospital after church with my portable Communion kit. I asked if she wished to receive Communion, and the light that had been missing from her eyes for a few days returned as she said, "Oh, yes." Another neighbor had been sitting with her, and I, of course, asked her to join us in Communion. The latter lady and her husband faithfully participate in church services but in a tradition without frequent

51

Communion and with no practice of Communion outside of those services.

By the next morning when I went to the pool for my morning swim, the entire community was abuzz with stories about Holy Communion in a hospital room!! The same type "buzz" happened last December when we had our first "Blue Christmas" service. When I entered the resort office the morning after that service, one of the staff said to me, "That was the most beautiful service last night. We really needed that." Interesting and a bit of a shock to hear her say that since she had not been present. She had not attended, but the word quickly spread from those who had participated. Once more I realized that the impact of our ministry of presence reaches far more than we know.

Not only do residents of the host resort participate in these services on Sunday and at other times, but others from surrounding resort communities participate. The presence of our community of faith and the stories of the impact of our community's ministry of prayer and caring impact the neighborhood in profound ways—including so many ways known only to God.

Senior adults do search for meaning and purpose. Some try to cope with loneliness and anxieties through activities—some more healthy than others. Along with water aerobics, yoga, book clubs, and photography, painting, and knitting classes, some also engage in less healthy pursuits of alcohol and casino visits.

Harold G. Koenig makes the observation that

> Americans have so much more than most people
> in the world, yet they often feel that they do not
> have enough. That's because a person's "need"
> is not filled by acquiring more things, more toys,
> more money, but rather than giving to and
> investing in the lives of others. . . .Spirituality is
> motivating, energizing, and inspiring, so
> developing spiritually can make a real difference
> during retirement. (34)

The Compline Years provide the elderly with time and
space for reflection; and those who did not develop an inner
life of faith in earlier years may yet find the joy of living in
the Light of God's love and may indeed find that new heart.

Parker Palmer expresses this idea:

> When we are young and wholly engaged with
> the external world, we may manage to feel
> "alive" for a while without an inner life. But
> when we experience diminishments and
> defeats—the kind that can come at any age and
> are inevitable when we get old—we run the risk
> of feeling dead before our time if we lack inner
> resources. (35)

When the church offers ways for the elderly to develop and live that inner life, both the church community and the individual grow.

Parker Palmer also relates this story:

> A disciple asks the rebbe: "Why does Torah tell us to 'place these words upon your hearts'?" Why does it not tell us to place these holy words in our hearts?' The rebbe answers: "It is because as we are, our hearts are closed, and we cannot place the holy words in our hearts. So we place them on top of our hearts. And there they stay until, one day, the heart breaks and the words fall in."—Hassidic Tale" (36)

When the elderly (and the entire community of faith) go into the neighborhood after gathering at God's table, nourished by the Eucharistic meal and continually strengthened by domestic church/monastic rituals, the elderly go out as evangelists to meet those who seek a new heart.

Writing concerning "new opportunities for meaning and significance" in retirement, Harold Koenig describes the map for how this new heart works as well as the ministry of Senior Evangelists:

> Spirituality can provide the older person with direction (where to go), power (the ability to go), and wisdom (how to go). . . .Spirituality gives life and focus. Spirituality helps to direct

attention to the needs in the world, needs that a person may have the gifts and talents to fulfill." (37)

Now, read the above quotation substituting "new heart" for "spirituality":

A new heart can provide the older person with direction (where to go), power (the ability to go), and wisdom (how to go). . . .*A new heart* gives life and focus. *A new heart* helps to direct attention to the needs in the world, needs that a person may have the gifts and talents to fulfill." (37)

Those who seek and find a new heart in God's light and love then join with all in faith as we pray:

May I live each day with fullness of mind,

Attending to life and all she places before me.

Thus will I live without hesitation.

Only then can I lie down in peace,

Having given life my all. (38)

Reflection:

Old age is not the ideal stage for the creation de nova of spiritual maturity. Persons must, however, begin from whatever level of spiritual development they bring to the last stage of life. Spiritual maturation is the developmental task that confronts the final stage of life.

> *--Elizabeth MacKinlay, et al, Aging, Spirituality and Pastoral Care: A Multi-National Perspective*

1. What life events or experiences might cause a person to seek a life of faith during the Compline Years?

2. How do we prepare to support and enable new (or re-discovered) faith in older people?

3. How do we prepare to become Senior Evangelists and to guide others in belonging, belief, and behavior?

Prayer: Create in us, Loving God, hearts filled with your love and a desire to share that love. Strengthen us, we pray, that we may show your love to all who seek a new heart. Amen.

The Elder as Evangelist

Lord God, you have called your servants to ventures of which we cannot see the ending, by paths as yet unknown. Give us faith to go out with good courage, not knowing where we go, but only that your hand is leading us and your love supporting us.

–The Lutheran Liturgy of Evening Prayer

While I had not thought about the T.E.L. Sunday School class ladies in a very long time, memories of Miss Henderson have and do pop up in my thinking from time to time. Miss Montez Henderson served as our junior high school librarian and taught seventh grade honors English.

As a voracious reader from a very young age, I looked forward to the weekly visits to the city library from the time I received my first library card when I was in the second grade. Entering junior high school meant that I suddenly had a library available every school day, and I eagerly explored and used the library. Librarians, of course, love to foster such enthusiasm; so Miss Henderson and I interacted often in the library plus in the seventh grade classroom.

She taught, guided, and encouraged me during that first year of junior high school, but the major and most lasting/continuing teaching she brought to my life came later and with only a slowly evolving recognition and thankfulness on my part.

I entered high school, and I don't remember any interactions with her; and she may have retired shortly after my junior high years. The next contact from her came years later. Somehow, she kept up with me (and certainly others, of course), and a lovely (both in content and elegant handwriting) congratulatory note from her arrived by mail shortly after my high school graduation, college graduation, seminary graduation, and on a couple of other occasions in my early professional life.

Today, social media enables us to remain in contact with friends, former students, former colleagues, and others around the world. We have extensive and frequent contact, and we respond immediately. Miss Henderson obviously scoured the home-town newspaper for notices concerning former students, and I imagine she kept a supply of lovely notecards at hand. Her notes exuded thoughtfulness as well as a certain pride in the accomplishments of her students—and I hope she felt some sense of accomplishment in her part in our lives.

Now, in my own Compline Years, I realize how often my own responses to news and momentous life events from former students and others consist of a quick smiley face emoji!!

While I know nothing of Miss Henderson's faith practices and spiritual life, I am confident that she joins the T.E.L. ladies and others who surround me in that great cloud of witnesses. She acted as a Senior Evangelist and also gave me a gift which continues today. She taught me a way of actively encouraging others.

One of the great ministries of our resort-based congregation involves writing notes of support to the seminarians with whom I interact in the weekend program. As the semester moves toward the final weeks which include deadlines for papers and taking exams, I distribute the names of seminarians and professors along with notecards and envelopes to those in our congregation who wish to write notes of encouragement to the seminarians and professors.

While individuals write in their own styles, the notes include words of encouragement and assurances of prayers for those hectic days when seminarians juggle their work-week jobs, church work, family, and the end-of-semester seminary work.

Over and over, seminarians send messages of thanks along with photos of the notes surrounding the books and papers during the process of writing major papers and taking exams. The message from each seminarian always involves the "I couldn't have done this without your prayers and encouragement" statement.

At some point in the spring semester, members of our congregation make a "field trip" to the seminary for Saturday chapel and lunch; and they meet, share Eucharist, and then lunch with the seminarians they support with Sunday and daily prayers plus those end-of-semester notes.

Miss Henderson demonstrated one way a person in the Compline Years lives and works as God's evangelist. Our congregation continues this work in another time and place.

The work of the Senior Evangelist transcends time, place, and physical/mental abilities.

> Chaplain Beth Jackson-Jordon recounts the story
> of a frail woman confined to her bed in a
> nursing home, who found purpose and meaning
> in being a good listener to nurses' aides,
> housekeepers, and others who moved in and out

of her room each day to provide care. Such a shift disrupts the dichotomy between dependence and interdependence that does not rely on equality of physical capacity. God's call in older adulthood invites even those with frail bodies and minds to serve the neighbor, as caregiver and care-receiver are graced by one another's presence. (39)

When my college roommate and I met at our university for our forty-fifth-year class reunion, we arrived a day before the events began and went out to eat dinner that evening. When our food arrived, we paused to thank God for that food, and part of our prayer included a thanksgiving for "all those whose life and labor bring this meal to us". When we finished the prayer, a young lady who had been clearing the table adjacent to ours came to us and quietly said, "Thank you for that." We quickly realized that she who was doing one of the least attractive jobs in that place heard people praying for her and giving thanks for her life and work.

We pray together at church, and we have private prayer lives. However, what about the people around us who rarely, if ever, hear anyone pray for them?

Seniors who continue belonging in the faith community and continue to grow in faith go into the community to live and serve God as evangelists. Whatever the nature of the senior's neighborhood—from independent living to intense dependence upon others—the senior continues to show God's love through actions and prayers for those in the senior's presence.

Our Senior Evangelists know, as Schillebeeckx affirms, that "God's presence and action is mediated by human beings, made visible in men and women caring for each other". (40)

In our senior community, we use a liturgy "A Journey Just Begun" when a person must leave the physical location of our community--usually when the person can either no longer live independently or no longer make the seasonal trip to a second home in our community. This liturgy, included in the second section of this book, may be expanded/adapted for the person and community.

In this liturgy (used in our service of Holy Eucharist after the sermon), both the individual departing and the community reaffirm vows based on the Baptismal Covenant and promise continued service to God and each other in the Compline Years which to us as people of faith represents part of a "Journey Just Begun".

As the Compline Years now often extend 30 years or more with much of that time spent in good health, the elderly retain the opportunity to continue vital ministry while also having leisure time to commit to prayer, study, and action.

Spiritual director and counselor Kathleen Fischer expresses it beautifully when she writes,

"There are dimensions of the Gospel, aspects of love, courage, faith, and fidelity, which only the old can sacramentalize for the human community. From the perspective of faith, the later years provide the most intense and vivid revelation of the paradox of the heart of the Christian Gospel: that in losing our lives we somehow find them; that loss can be gain, and weakness, strength; that death is the path to life." (41)

Living at home, enjoying healthy, active retirement years or living in a care facility with declining physical/mental abilities, or some place in between these two situations, elders represent an opportunity for the church to engage in mutual ministry and to celebrate and foster continued mission and ministry.

The elder who engages in domestic church/monastic practices not only possesses a rich and growing inner spiritual life but also possesses and uses outward and visible symbols of that life and those practices. With those symbols visible in the home or other living space, those who visit see those symbols which become an opportunity for conversation and evangelism.

Reflection:

The challenge is not just to fill the retiree's time, but rather to meet needs with the talents and resources the retiree can provide. The vocational question is, "How can I respond to my neighbor's need where I am and with what I am."

--Arthur H. Becker, <u>Ministry with Older Persons</u>

1. Think of a person you know (past or present) who you would describe as a Senior Evangelist. How does that person live out her/his Baptismal promises?

2. How do you perceive yourself as one who is or will become a Senior Evangelist?

3. What spiritual practices do you currently employ or need to develop to enable you to be a Senior Evangelist?

Prayer: Ageless and Timeless Creator God, thank you for the lives and ministries of people of all ages. We thank you especially for the Senior Evangelists {who we now name. . . . . . .) and all those who remain unnamed whose lives and faith show us and the world around them your love. Amen.

RITUAL

Ritual helps people focus their lives to that they know what is real and important.

Rituals are special and engaging them involves leaving some things behind so we can attend to others.

--<u>Sacramental Living: Falling Stars & Coloring Outside the Lines</u>, Dwight and Linda Vogel.

Rituals. We all engage in rituals. Some we may name, but many more remain unnamed. My nephew, a high school football coach, uses the word "ritual" and can explain exactly what he and his team do before and after each game as "pre-game and post-game ritual." The coaches and players have developed a precise series of words, actions, and symbols which occur in a coordinated sequence.

Whether we use the word "ritual" or not, each of us might describe our own rituals. We have morning rituals—get out of bed, make a trip to the small room down the hall, brush teeth, drink coffee, pray, ... and on into the day.

Domestic church/monasticism depends upon ritual, for "ritual offers opportunity for reconnection that can enhance life purpose and change personal perspectives on being and living alone. Ritual can assist individuals to connect with both present and past experience." (42)

When elders develop and practice domestic church/ monastic practices in community with those with whom they regularly gather at God's table, they gain strength from the knowing that others join them in these prayers and practices no matter when or where they engage in the ritual. Thus, they live in the strength of belonging to God and to the spiritual community.

Belief involves both action and memory, and

> Participation in ritual can simultaneously move
> one forward and provide a sense of stability by

highlighting continuity. Through the use of ritual emotions can be discharged; identity can be shaped; connections can be developed or restored. (43)

Even when memory fails, elders benefit from rituals connected with faith. David Jackson states that

> to connect with faith and faith in God during spiritual care, prayer (e.g., group prayer, intercessory prayer) has been found to offer a sense of strength and comfort for older people living with dementia. . . Through reading scripture and the Bible (or equivalent), some older people remain connected to their faith and faith in God and are given strength and comfort. (44)

The football coaches and players develop and use rituals precisely for the positive results gained from those rituals; and our congregations benefit from developing rituals which extend throughout life. While this book deals with the needs of senior adults, the development and use of rituals needs to begin early.

We teach and reaffirm our baptismal vows on occasions throughout the church year and state that we will be "faithful in the Word, the Prayers, and the Sacraments", but many church members do not have a practice of reading Holy Scripture and prayer outside church services.

The young football players engage in rituals which end—at the end of the football season or the end of their high school days. However, they learn that actions and symbols have power and support their sense of community, and their early learning provides a foundation for continued formation and use of ritual.

Development of rituals for domestic church/monasticism provides an even greater strength of community and faith for a lifetime.

Researchers report:

> There is an absence of symbols of transcendence in our society that would enable persons to discover answers to questions related to the meaning of ageing and growing old. Symbols provide guideposts for persons as they move into the future, even into dying and death. A true symbol moves beyond itself, not only denoting something, but also suggesting that which is hidden. The hiddenness is not just buried in the past, but also contains a promise of the future. It captures the undiscovered "more" to which a symbol always points. It never simply escapes into the past, but always opens into the future. The ability to symbolize allows persons to transcend time boundaries, to reminiscence about the past and to anticipate the future. (45)

Developing domestic church/monastic practices reinforces faith through ritual. Ritual enables the elderly to recall, remember, and grow faith in this Compline of life.

Reflection:

All ritual carries a deep unspeakable desire for connection, relationship, meaning, even for transcendence.

--Diarmuid O'Murchu, Adult Faith, Growing in Wisdom and Understanding

1. How does the use of ritual and the symbols associated with ritual meet the desire for connection and relationship?

2. What rituals do we use to maintain connection and relationship?

3. What rituals could you develop and continue even when physical limitations may require many significant changes in your life?

Prayer: God of steadfast love, may our thoughts ever praise you; may our words always speak your love; may our hearts constantly seek you. Amen.

DOMESTIC CHURCH

But whenever you pray, go into your room and shut the

door and pray to your Father who is in secret; and your

Father who sees in secret will reward you.

--Matthew 6:6, NRSV

Engaging in the familiar behaviors of Christian life and the community of faith imbues elders with strength, resilience, and peace even when those behaviors take place in a new and different setting.

> Faith involves believing that persons are worthwhile, important, and of value, even if helpless and dependent on others, because God cares about and values every human being, regardless of their capacity to produce for society. Mature faith involves putting on positive attitudes and/or taking steps toward constructive action despite feelings to the contrary. . . . By reading scripture or other aids to devotion, spending time in personal prayer and meditation, and worshiping within a community of believers, persons nurture their relationship with God, . . . (46)

Domestic church/monastic practices which elders develop together in the community of faith may solidify and reinforce long-practiced behaviors with the added strength of knowing that others in the community join into the same practices. The Pew Research Center in the Religious Landscape Study finds that when the elderly continues the long-practiced behaviors connected with faith, these persons demonstrate:

> Improved confidence and self-esteem; restored relationships; a more hopeful outlook; a higher

sense of purpose and meaning; a greater sense of personal dignity. (47)

While many abilities diminish or end prior to the end of earthly life, research shows that "even with advancing cognitive impairment, the ability to participate in relationship with God is one of the last human capacities to be lost before consciousness itself ceases." (48)

Sister Joan Chittister describes behaviors in the Compline of life:

> Finally, as we grow older, when we begin the last stage of life, it is clear that behaviors and failures are not the stuff of religion much anymore. Now, the ecstasy of life and the surrender to the Mystery become the last of the revelations of religion. Now everything we learned long ago, gave up to some degree long ago, never left completely long ago, begins to make sense. Begins to become me. Begins my new beginning as a person. It is the older members of society who not only teach us how to live. They teach us how to die, how to make sense of the unity between life and death, how to love life without fearing death—because we know ourselves to have been always on the way, even when we did not know where we were going. (49)

In this Compline of life, the elderly may demonstrate fully the depth of Ruth Duck's understanding as she writes about Don Saliers' "thought concerning how, as we bring our 'humanity at full stretch before God' over time, prayer and worship form us in Christian character and transform us through God's self-communication in Christ." (51) Indeed, one might well describe this Compline of life as the time when all of one's being lives "at full stretch before God" and demonstrates that depth of faith to all who will learn from this continued living out of full, active participation.

Ideally, we would support the development of domestic church practices for everyone at every age and stage of life— young, single people; couples; families with children; extended families living together; friends sharing housing; and senior adults in all types of living situations. The Roman Catholic Church in more modern times defined "domestic church":

> The term "Domestic Church" refers to the family, the smallest body of gathered believers in Christ. Though recovered only recently, the term dates all the way back to the first century AD. The Greek word *ecclesiola* referred to "little church." Our Early Church Fathers understood that the home was fertile ground for discipleship, sanctification, and holiness. (52)

According to the Second Vatican Council's Dogmatic Constitution on the Church: "The family, is so to speak, the domestic church. This means that it is in the context of the family that we first learn who God is and to prayerfully seek His will for us". (53)

The Catholic Church furthermore provides some ideas for building "domestic church" which the elderly, as well as others, may adapt for use. These include:

- Praying and reading from Scripture daily, certainly before meals, but also first thing in the morning or before bed.

- Demonstrate love for family, friends, neighbors, and the world. Remind those around you that God loves them and has given them gifts to serve others.

- Talk freely about the presence of God in the joys and sorrows of your life.

- Allow those around you to witness your practice of domestic church/monasticism. Encourage those around you to pray daily on their own, to listen for and respond to God's call. (54)

Contemporary writing and instruction regarding Domestic Church tend to stress Domestic Church as a practice for families consisting of parents and children. Ideally, the domestic church practice begins early in life but may also begin at any age or stage of life.

However, we must also recognize and acknowledge a wide variety of domestic settings. J.M. Bennett addresses the subject of contemporary households:

> . . .I now bring this whole conversation into contact with our twenty-first century question about "what kind of family is needed for the 'domestic' church". First and foremost, I want to suggest that the term "family" in question does not do very much work, for from the vision I have discussed here, a primary Christian vision of family is, quite simply, the church. I prefer to use the term household, or perhaps "daily household" or "local household" . . .because local household is a term that is more in line with the kind of witness that Christians have. (55)

By acknowledging and blessing the local or daily household in all settings and situations--the always-single, divorced, widowed; the home-owner, the apartment-dweller, the RV camper; the room in assisted living, or the hospital room—we honor the spirit of God within those who live out their Baptisms for all of life and in any and all domestic settings.

Bennett continues his discussion of households with more descriptions:

> Furthermore, . . .over the course of their lives, people . . . experience a series of very different living situations. They belong, at the least, to a biological family of origin, but sometimes children have more than one family of origin, for example, those who grow up in a foster home. Many people establish one or more different families that merge into one another over time. People often live alone for phases of their lives, especially in old age. Finally they may live in collective settings such a homes for the aged or assisted living. (56)

Many elders have experienced changes in living situations, and our communities of faith may appropriately respond to these changes via the continuity of faith community expressed in domestic church/monastic practices. "In their varied family relationships, the faithful need a church that, based on the sacrament of baptism, acknowledges their individual divine calls, supports them, and integrates them structurally and theologically within the self-understanding of the church." (57)

Both St. John Chrysostom and St. Augustine write using the term "domestic church", and we have the opportunity to learn from their ancient thoughts and wisdom and to adapt and apply these precepts in our modern age.

St. John Chrysostom in his domestic church writings "focuses on helping Christians develop virtues. . . . Chrysostom proposed a program of Christian living 'inspired by the monastic ideal'. . . ." (58) By developing domestic church practices, members of our faith communities enter the Compline Years with a firm foundation of inner strength even when much around them changes.

St. Augustine directly addressed the household situation of a widow:

> . . .in a letter to a widow named Juliana,
> Augustine mentions 'holy widowhood' as
> similar to living a life of vowed . . .
> monasticism, so that Juliana's holy widowhood
> is a distinctive kind of household. It is not a
> traditional family, for Juliana lives with at least
> one other widow, but still, hers is a household
> that gets the designation 'domestic church' and
> not the more traditional 'nuclear family'. (59)

The living arrangements of care facilities and retirement centers might be the present-day version of Juliana's life with other widows or widowers. Furthermore, household/family composition in our society reflects an almost infinite number of configurations.

By affirming the vision of Christian family as the church, those who engage in domestic church practices gain even more strength of belief, continued belonging, behaviors of a life of faith which extend and enlarge the life and witness of the faith community into households and neighborhoods.

We who believe that nothing can separate us from God's love have the opportunity and responsibility to build a vision of church (faith community) that expands and continues even when (especially when!) the elder's life situation takes the elder away from the regular, physical location of community worship.

While the elder may engage in domestic church practices alone, she/he remains connected to the community by using the same prayers and symbols that others use. One mission for the faith community includes continually providing those present and those in settings away from the gathered community with prayer requests and devotional materials. A mission for those not physically present during regular worship services includes not only prayers for the community but communication and assurance of those continued prayers.

Domestic church practices, BEING the church wherever the elder finds him/herself require an understanding of church which does extend and expand. One's vocation continues for life even when the nature and perhaps the location of the vocation changes.

The teaching that one belongs to God through baptism and to the community of faith lived out together in our royal priesthood enables members of the community to continue to grow spiritually and to live out vocation for all of life.

Thinking once again about The Eldest Ladies' Sunday School class from my teen years—yes, I firmly believe that they prayed for me. The domestic church practices of those ladies continue, via the power of the Holy Spirit, to impact the world today and beyond today.

Reflection:

Both Augustine and John Chrysostom (who each use the term "domestic church") are paying careful attention to an alternate reality that new Christians enter into as they are baptized.

People living in their differing family relationship want a church that does not treat them simply as objects of pastoral concern, but as the subjects of their faith.

--Thomas Kniepts, et al, <u>The Household of God and Local Households, Revisiting the Domestic Church</u>

1. How do domestic church practices support living out Baptismal promises?

2. What different "local household" settings have you experienced in your life?

3. How do pastoral needs and faith practices change as "local household" circumstances change?

Prayer: Mother/Father God, bless, comfort, and strengthen our homes in all their many configurations and changes. May the prayers and worship in our home rise as incense to praise and thank you; and may the Holy Spirit give us wisdom and strength to share your love both in our homes and to all we encounter. We ask in the name of the one who shared the gentle hospitality of household and home with Mary, Martha, and Lazarus in Bethany. Amen.

MONASTICISM

This life therefore is not righteousness, but growth in righteousness, not health, but healing, not being but becoming, not rest but exercise. We are not yet what we shall be, but we are growing toward it, the process is not yet finished, but it is going on, this is not the end, but it is the road. All does not yet gleam in glory, but all is being purified. — **Martin Luther**

Monasticism: Read or say the word, and a media-inspired picture may explode into one's brain—a picture of a brown-robed person holding a quill pen while hunched over a writing desk or perhaps a group of such persons holding up the robe edges while stomping grapes! In more sedate thought-pictures, perhaps we visualize a chapel of the brown-robed people chanting Gregorian liturgies.

While at least some of the latter still exists in present-day monastic orders, religious orders today exist in many forms—from the cloistered to those who belong to communities while living and working in the secular world and those who use monastic practices individually. In fact, the earliest monastics did not belong to a religious order.

> Actually there was no such thing (religious order) in early Christianity. There was only monasticism. Many men, and some women, sought to save their souls by taking up a life of prayer, either alone or in communities of like-minded people. (60)

In our faith communities, individuals who develop monastic practices form a firm foundation of life which Christopher Jamison, the Abbot of Worth, describes:

> One way of surviving the torrent of modern living other than by going with the flow is the monastic way of life. It offers not only monks

but also laypeople a series of stepping stones to help us keep our footing when the current is flowing strongly. Stepping stones are not a destination and they are not a technique, but they can help to steady our stride, giving us the confidence to keep traveling. (61)

Using the stepping stone image may assist elders in developing and using monastic practices because the Compline Years bring time to continue spiritual development while at the same time experiencing the losses and anxieties which come with advanced years. Stepping stones give sure footing along walkways or in streams, and elders need spiritual stepping stones for navigating often difficult pathways in the Compline years.

The father of the monastic way of life which continues today, St. Benedict, wrote the famous <u>Rule of Benedict</u>.

In the Prologue to the Rule of St. Benedict, he writes: '. . .as we progress in this way of life and in faith, we shall run on the path of God's commandments, our hearts overflowing with the inexpressible delight of love. (62)

Monastic practices enable the elderly to develop and use practices which Goldsmith identifies as important for continuity of worship and the use of familiar signs and symbols as part of "that which has the capacity to create forms of worship that tap into spiritual memory." (63)

The Abbot of Worth provides a description of monastic prayer in a simple statement which directly addresses the formation of such practices for use in domestic church. He encourages this practice and describes monastic prayer as

> the carving out of sacred time and space
> dedicated to rejoicing in the goodness of God
> and repenting of the thoughts that impede that
> goodness in my life. So try to create a sacred
> space at home, maybe something as simple as an
> icon, and build a time of quiet into the day, a
> time to visit the sacred space. (64)

While the resident Benedictine orders continue around the world, Paul Wilkes, who made regular visits to a monastery, provides us with a helpful idea of Benedict's vision of monastic life:

> When Benedict bid his followers to make a vow
> of stability, he wisely did not attach it to
> something as abstract as an institution, namely
> the religious orders that would eventually carry
> his name. Benedict saw that holiness would be
> found not so much by searching for a perfect
> haven to inhabit or having the right religious
> affiliation, but in the giving of oneself to a

specific place: to its transformation and to one's own. (65)

Monastic practices in the domestic church setting enable the elderly to engage in the lament birthed by the losses and suffering involved in aging while holding fast to faith for oneself and the community in the present time of the Compline Years and for the journey just begun. A person using monastic practices does indeed transform her/himself and the place the person sets aside for daily spiritual growth practices.

Gordon Lathrop expresses this faith and hope in terms of liturgical life:

> Christian liturgical life rehearses and
> participates in the truth about human suffering—
> to practice a liturgical *ars moriendi* (art of
> dying) without morbidity or denial of life. . . . It
> holds honestly about what befalls us and the
> hope beyond all ills as figured in the divine
> *kenosis*. (66)

Monastic practices which elders develop together in the community of faith may solidify and reinforce long-practiced behaviors (and newly formed rituals) with the added strength of knowing that others in the community join into the same practices.

The writers in <u>The Study of Liturgy</u> observe the vocation that retirees and others now find in the use of daily personal monastic-style practices which many traditionally viewed as something belonging to clergy.

> When clergy of any church recite the office, or its equivalent, they are not only enjoying a special personal intimacy with God, or a stimulating exercise comparable with jogging; they are bringing the praises and petitions of the whole body. Even when they have to do this alone. . ., they are still the minimum congregation for that worship at that moment. They are not acting instead of the Church, or supplying other people's defects. There is indeed a ministry of extended worship, a place for those who can give more time to worship than most are able to do. In addition to communities and orders and clergy, many retired people and others are finding that they have a vocation of this sort. (67

Monastic practices provide the elderly (and others) with a structure and form for this vocation of prayer and spiritual growth.

From birth, our lives have structure. We begin with the eat, sleep, eat, sleep cycles and move into eat, play, sleep. When our school days begin, our lives develop a structure that continues in various forms through our working lives.

Retirement arrives with, for many, a complete loss of structure which may result in a deep sense of loss and uncertainty and sometimes results in unhealthy or even destructive habits. On the other hand, think of the news stories we hear or read from time to time about a person, often over 80 or even over 90, who now celebrates a long-desired university degree or who engages in body-building competitions or marathons. The interviews accompanying these stories usually carry a theme—this person completed his/her professional work life and, for some, raising children, and made a decision for some type of intense, specialized growth.

These examples demonstrate intellectual and physical growth and development, and elders who develop and practice spiritual growth via monasticism probably will not appear in the news but will certainly experience the growth of inner life as well as ministry with and to others.

Elders who embrace monastic practices continue a long tradition of lay people seeking a deeper spiritual life.

> Monasticism addresses what is fundamental to a human being. Reflecting again on monasticism's origins, it was comforting to remember that this way of life was not the creation of medieval bishops or theologians trying to so institutionalize belief that it could be more efficiently monitored. Christian monasticism sprang from a deep yearning in lay people, opening their arms and hearts to the love

of God so that the aching deep within could be healed, and the uncertainty of the human condition—if not resolved—at least be boldly faced. (68)

Monastic practices continue a life-long need for structure while also providing strength and purpose. Greg Peters explores the "monastic foundation of Christian spirituality" in The Monkhood of All Believers and asserts that "Since its advent, monasticism has been an integral part of the Church, because it expresses a spiritual norm that is *universal*, a normative value for every believer." (69)

Paul Wilkes observes: "Lay people are entering the monastic world and carrying their experiences there into the world outside. Oblate groups linked to monasteries are springing up all over the country." (70) The lay people described here represent those who seek out a religious community, spend time in that community, and then take on vows regarding the practices of those communities (including reading Scripture, praying, and serving God in the community) in order to be an "oblate" or associate of the community.

By including education and resources for monastic practices, every faith community provides members of the community with the opportunity for developing a rich and ever-deepening spiritual life.

The monastic practices of elders enable elders to both speak honestly to the tensions of the Compline of life as well as to exercise a certain autonomy in their spiritual lives and practices at a time when they may have little autonomy in other areas of life.

People who enter traditional monastic life give up worldly goods to enter a new type of life. The life of older adults often mirrors some of the giving up without the dimension of personal choice to do so. The "giving up" frequently includes departure from the family home; restrictions concerning diet; surrendering time management (meal times set by others; medical appointments dictate schedules); loss of privacy (living in a care facility or with family members); loss of autonomy (inability to drive); and diminishment of physical abilities (eyesight, hearing, mobility).

In this Compline of life, losses and the giving up process loom large in the lives of the elderly. However, monastic practices provide the elderly with a powerful structure for continued faith and belonging. Andrea Sherman, co-founder and president of Transitional Keys, speaks of the power of ritual which monastic practices bring to life: "In a nutshell, rituals provide a framework to symbolically mark changes that occur in life, knitting us into the greater fabric of ourselves, our family and community." (71) Furthermore, she asserts that ritual provides "order and clarity in times of change; relief and comfort in times of anxiety; integration and healing in times of loss; and continuity and community in times of reflection and celebration." (72)

For elders who live with and lament the losses which occur with age and also seek to live the baptismal covenant for all of life, the ritual of monastic practices provides a firm foundation for continued faithfulness, growth, and community.

Dwight Vogel avows:

> If the baptismal covenant is a life-long process, then our faith and understanding about God are meant to be dynamic. Familiar words learned since childhood can play an important role in sustaining Christian identity, but continued learning and growth keeps our faith from being static, frozen at the point we were baptized or affirmed the baptismal covenant for ourselves. As a full range of scriptural imagery for God is explored in Christian worship, believers continue on a journey beyond all words and knowledge. As the baptismal journey of faith continues, Christians experience God in the midst of their lives which inspires new ways of witness and service. (73)

Monastic practices provide elders with strength, with stepping stones, comfort, peace, and continued spiritual growth in the Compline years.

Reflection:

But whenever you pray, go into your room and shut the door and pray to your Father who is in secret; and your Father who sees in secret will reward you.

--Mathew 6:6 NRSV

What is a monastery? A monastery is not so much a place set apart for monks and nuns as it is a place set apart, period.

--Ronald Rolheiser, Domestic Monastery

1. In your home, how do you set apart a place for prayer and other monastic practices?

2. What signs and symbols do you use to set apart such a place?

3. How do those signs and symbols make this a sacred place for you and also connect you to others in your faith community (and perhaps the faithful around the world)?

4. How are your signs, symbols, and practices portable—i.e., if you were hospitalized or in a care facility, how would you continue your monastic practices?

Prayer: We pray, Lord, that everything we do may be prompted by your inspiration, so that every prayer and work of ours may begin from you and be brought by you to completion. Amen.

--based on the Prologue to St. Benedict's <u>Prayer Book for Beginners</u>

THE COMPLINE YEARS

PART OF

A JOURNEY JUST BEGUN

Peace be to the whole community, and love with faith, from God the Father and the Lord Jesus Christ. Grace be with all who have an undying love for our Lord Jesus Christ.
–Ephesians 6:23 NRSV

Days, weeks, months, or even years prior to physical death, faithful Christians in our parishes depart from our shared Table and community of faith gathered in worship simply to exit stage right and disappear from our sight and spiritual care. Perhaps, on a Sunday soon after the "exit, stage right", members of the congregation learn that a beloved member of the community now resides in a care facility after a fall or now lives with a family member in a distant location. Gradual declines in health allow some to engage in planning and participate in decision-making related to the move away from independent living.

Developing and practicing domestic church/monastic practices supports the elderly in their lives of belonging, belief, and behavior all their days. These rituals sustain them in their lives of faith and service even when they can no longer be physically present in their home church and allow elders to take practices and symbols with them at a time of great loss and change.

Rather than Wilder's depiction of the silent exit through the dark, stage right portal, the elder's departure from the home community of faith should be marked with prayer and blessing and assurance of continual shared domestic church/ monastic practices.

Archibald MacLeish in his Pulitzer Prize winning play J.B. retells the Biblical story of Job in a modern setting.

> In the Biblical story, Job asks, "Why?" But no satisfactory answer to his question emerges—

not from the confrontation with the three comforters, not from the arguments of Elihu, nor from the framing device of Satan's wager, not even from the voice in the whirlwind. . . . The beauty and power of the biblical story of Job depend finally not on reasoned answers but rather on an act of faith. (74)

In the Compline of life, elders often ask, "why?" and learn again the ancient lesson of life as lived not dependent upon the reasoned answers but upon faith.

In the closing scene of the drama, Sarah, J.B.'s wife, approaches him with an unlit lantern and laments the darkness by observing that the candles in the church have burned out. J.B. responds from his deep faith:

Then blow on the coal of the heart.

The Candles in churches are out.

The lights have gone out in the sky.

Blow on the coal of the heart

And we'll see by and by. (75)

J.B. challenges Sarah to light the lantern she carries with her love but instead lights the lantern himself as Sarah rests her head on his shoulder. Then J.B. and Sarah rise and look into the darkness of their home. J.B. remarks that it is too dark to see. Sarah then replies that one must trust in love to see, for love is "all the light now". (76)

As the shadows fall in the Compline of life, elders seek light. Like Sarah who approached J.B. with the unlit lantern, elders look to the One who is Light and Life. Christ, our Light, shines in all our hearts. Like Sarah who leans her head on J.B.'s shoulder, the elder leans into the comfort, strength, and wisdom of the Holy Spirit and continues on this journey just begun.

A JOURNEY JUST BEGUN

One congregation's journey into domestic

church/monastic practices.

This section describes an on-going, ever-evolving living out of belonging, belief, and behavior for one congregation of people living in their Compline Years with a vision of this stage of life as part of our Journey Just Begun in God's love and light.

Through sharing our own experiences and resources, we hope to inspire and enable other congregations and groups to use these practices; improve upon them; tailor them in all the ways specific to local demographics, worship styles, cultures, and more; and, above all, give this part of mission and ministry to the Holy Spirit for empowerment with life and energy.

This ministry in our congregation began in Advent (a great time for anticipation and beginnings, of course!). Over the four Sundays of Advent, members of our congregation received an item each Sunday plus written resources for use in their own domestic church/monastic practices.

Around the luncheon table, we discussed the items which became outward and visible symbols--shared symbols for use in our personal domestic church/monastic rituals. We discussed the idea of domestic church/monasticism and how we would use these practices as part of our continuing as a community even when we cannot be physically together. Our seasonal members especially embraced the idea of community even when apart.

After our initial Advent Study time, new members of the congregation received the same items during lunch times when those now experienced in the use of domestic church/monastic practices shared the items, the symbolism and use of each item, and their own experiences of deepening faith and sense of community via domestic church/ monasticism.

The Notebook

On the first Sunday of Advent, each person received a small 3-ring binder (in this case, half-sheet sized binders which include some dividers and pockets for additional items such as a pen, prayer cards, or other small items). The binder provides a system of organization in a size large enough for easy handling and small enough for portability and ease of placement in an area designated for domestic church/ monastic practices.

The binders on this first Sunday of Advent included printed materials which began with the Baptismal Covenant. Each Sunday during that Advent plus during the seasons of Lent and Advent in subsequent years, everyone receives prayers and/or short readings appropriate for the season.

In addition, world and local events bring occasions for specific prayers and/or meditations as additions to the notebooks. The notebook dividers allow each person to organize prayers and readings for personal use, and the 3-ring-binder format allows people to add their own material.

Our initial discussion of domestic church/monastic practices also included the elements of setting aside a time and place for daily prayer and the use of symbols as a way to designate the domestic church space as well as a reminder that we share some of these symbols as a sign of continued community even when we are apart. Although we may pray alone, we also pray together.

The Shell

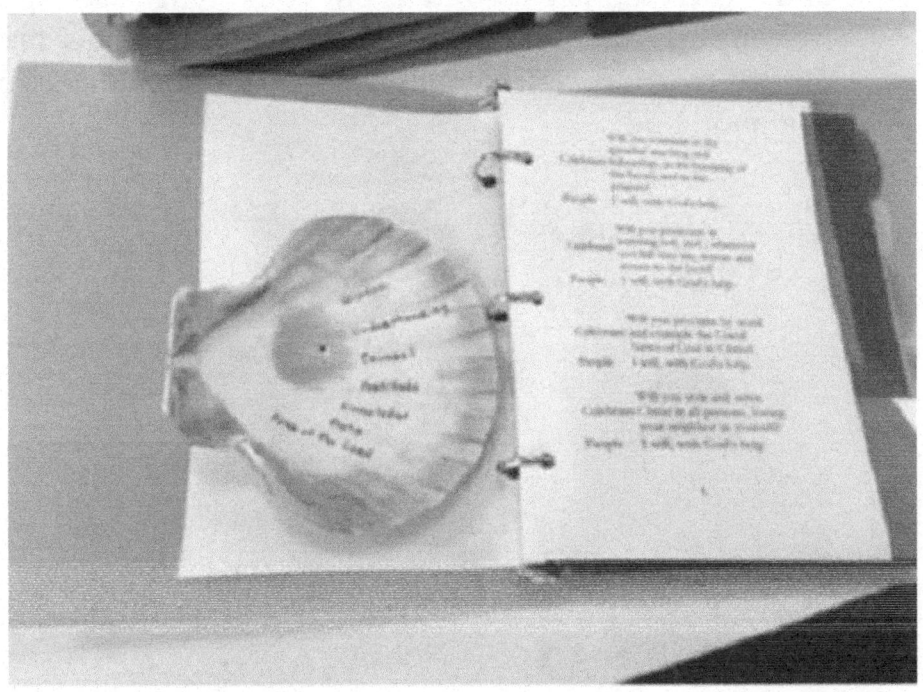

On the first Sunday of Advent along with the notebook containing the Baptismal Covenant, each person also received a shell (a 4-inch clam shell). After reading our baptismal promises, we discussed the symbolism of the shell—often used in baptisms. Each person then used a permanent marker to write the gifts of the Holy Spirit on the inside of the shell and added notebook pages with the Isaiah 11:2-3 listing of the Gifts of the Spirit.

Our discussion included ways to use this shell to remind us of our own baptism as well as our community of people who live out the baptismal promises—and as a reminder that the gifts of the Holy Spirit continue to flow through us into our neighborhood.

Link, the Prayer-Pal Panda

Like good stewards of the manifold grace of God, serve one

another with whatever gift each of you has received.

--I Peter 4:10 NRSV

On the second Sunday of our Advent study, our reflections centered specifically on our community; and we distributed stuffed pandas wearing a t-shirt with our chapel logo. This first introduction of the Panda to the community became a powerfully intense moment of Holy Spirit-filled grace.

The hands reaching out to receive the Panda quickly hugged the Panda to a position as close to the heart as possible. These Senior Evangelists gathered around the table (both the Eucharistic table and luncheon table) that day hugged the Pandas close, and then the tears began to flow.

The Panda provides each person with a symbol of our community at all times and in all places. One of our group named the Panda "Link" in order to remind us of the spiritual link we celebrate. Link provides each person with an outward and visible symbol of this prayerful faith community, and Link provides an easily transportable, warm, fuzzy item which we soon learned brings comfort to many.

Soon after Link came to be part of our domestic settings, Del, a retired priest in his late 80's, arrived early one Sunday morning with a story to share. He had received a call during the previous week from an old friend—a lady with whom he became friends more than 70 years ago when they were high school cheerleaders together in Nebraska.

Del said that his friend called and asked what he was doing.

Del replied, "I'm sitting here with Link."

The friend then asked, "Who is Link?"

Del shared what we were doing in our faith community with domestic church/monastic practices and the symbols we use. He told his friend that when he went to bed at night, Link went into the bedroom with him. Then, when he got up in the morning, he took Link into the kitchen with him as he made coffee and began his daily prayers; and then he took Link into the living room where Del would read or watch movies.

He said, "I told her that I am never alone because of Link—because Link reminds me of the faith community I love."

His friend replied, "I wish I had something like that."

When Del finished his story, I responded with the idea that she could certainly have Link live with her, too. His eyes sparkled with delight as he accepted another panda, and he shipped his friend her very own Link that week.

On another Sunday after our service, one of our Senior Evangelists saw a lady sitting at one of the poolside tables. The lady, a recent widow, was alone and eagerly accepted the invitation to join us for lunch; and she attended every Sunday service during her month-long stay at the resort. She happily accepted Link as her companion, and she came to church one Sunday with the story of her next-door neighbor who received a diagnosis of serious and terminal illness that week

110

and was leaving for treatment in a place closer to family. She said, "I gave Link to her. She needed him." Of course, we added her neighbor to our prayers and provided a replacement panda for this dear lady who responded unselfishly to the need of her neighbor.

Quite often, we receive requests from people asking to purchase a panda after meeting Link (and hearing Link's story) in a neighbor's home. We do not sell the pandas but freely provide a panda to anyone who asks, and we celebrate this aspect of our Senior Evangelists who demonstrate 'linking" up with God's mission in our neighborhood.

Link now lives in houses, apartments, extended care facilities, recreational vehicles, sometimes in hospital rooms, and wherever our community lives and travels. Link travels via air, by rail, in recreational vehicles, in automobiles, and even in golf carts!

The Prayer Beads

Likewise the Spirit helps us in our weakness; for we do not know how to pray as we ought, but that very Spirit intercedes with sighs too deep for words.

—Romans 8:26 NRSV

On the third Sunday of Advent, we continue our growing into a community of faith practicing domestic church and learning monastic practices. Some members of our faith community grew up in the church and have used domestic church practices in their families and now, in most of their living situations, continue those practices alone.

However, an increasing number have entered the faith community after many years away or having never engaged in a life of faith. We use prayer beads as an outward and visible symbol and as an aid to guided prayer (and, for some, the development of a prayer life).

Jesus' disciples asked him to "teach us TO pray" not "how to" pray. Surely, they knew the pattern of Jewish prayers, but they also saw Jesus taking time for prayer and would have heard him praying, so they asked, "Lord, teach us to do that thing that you do".

In her writing concerning "Prayer in Solitude", Julia Gatta describes the creation of physical space for prayer:

> Creating a sacred space for ourselves, even if it consists of a corner of our room, or habitually returning to the same location, generates an atmosphere conducive to prayer. Returning to this hallowed place sets in motion, at subliminal levels of our consciousness, a readiness for prayer. (77)

While domestic church/monastic practices ideally include the setting aside time and space for prayer, changes in the elder's life often dictate the need for simplification. A person confined to a bed will not be able to move to another designated space for prayer; but through learned and practiced domestic church/monasticism, the person makes sacred any space and time for prayer.

The use of the prayer beads which each person receives on the third Sunday of Advent enables the person to continue a familiar ritual again with the knowledge that others in the community use the same symbol and engage in the same practices. For a person experiencing memory loss or a time of extreme illness and weakness, holding the beads may bring comfort in ways we can only entrust to God to know and the Holy Spirit to sanctify.

For anyone, the person with long experience in prayer or the person searching for a way to begin to pray, the prayer beads provide both symbol of community prayers and a way to guide private prayers. Some, of course, may wish to use a Rosary; and continued use of domestic church/monastic practices easily opens the way for a discussion of and practice with the use of a Rosary (plus more printed prayers and prayer guides for the Domestic Church/ Monasticism notebook).

To facilitate the community's domestic church/monastic practices, we provide copies of *Forward Day by Day* for each person; and on this Sunday, we look again at our Baptismal promise to be faithful in our prayers, and each person receives the prayer beads.

In the simple design we use, the beads form a chain with colored beads plus beads with the letters spelling ACTS. The chain also includes an end clip which allows the person to attach the prayer chain to the notebook or to a place of her/his choosing.

Handout pages for the notebook include the guide for using the prayer chain.

The letter "A" represents Adoration, and our notebook prayer guide includes examples of prayers of adoration followed by examples of prayers for each of the next three letters:

"C" brings us to prayers of confession

"T" reminds us to engage in a time of thanksgiving to God

"S" may represent "supplication" or, using a simpler term, "stuff"

Our guide for this last letter encourages people to use this time to pray for those in our community, the world, the environment, and to include the day's news as an additional focus of prayers.

The Cross

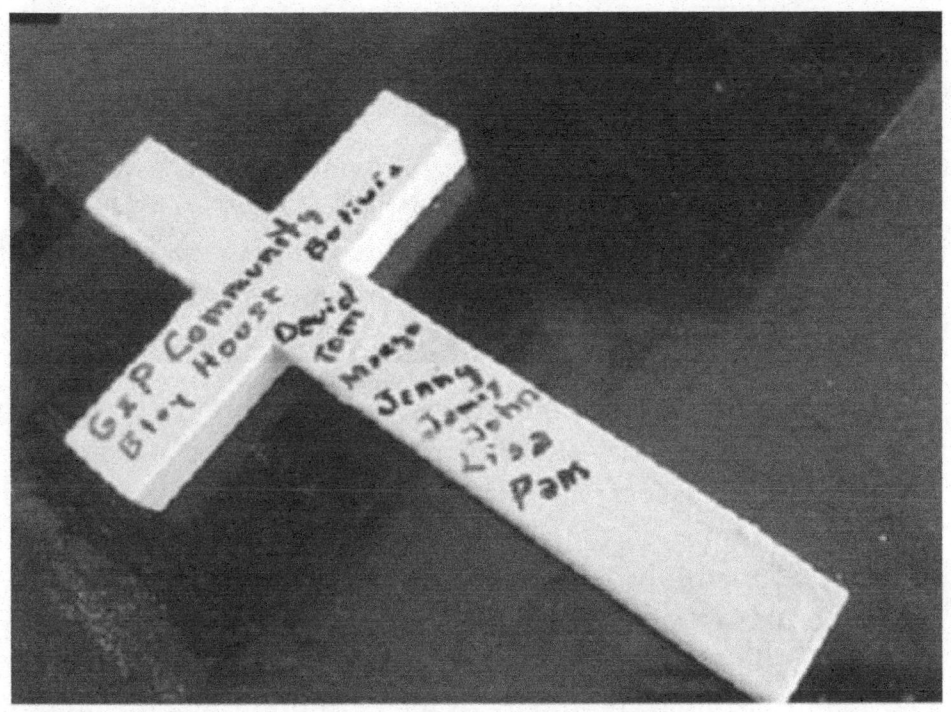

Live in the joy and peace of the divine Majesty. Live lost in divine love. Live for divine love and of divine love. Oh cherished cross! Through thee my most bitter trials are replete with graces.

--St. Paul of the Cross

116

We wear crosses and display them in our homes as well as in our churches as the symbol of God entering into our suffering; God's love triumphant in the lifting up of Jesus on the cross; and Jesus showing the Kingdom of God lifted up and at work in both present and future.

On the fourth Sunday of Advent, we focus on the symbolism of the cross; and each person receives a 12-inch tall wooden cross coated with white dry-erase paint. These crosses provide another outward and visible sign for each person's domestic church space in the home.

We make the commitment to write prayer requests on the crosses with dry-erase pens and to pray for "whatever is on all the crosses." The latter commitment assures all in this community of faith of the prayers of others even when those prayers might not be communicated in person or aloud. Requests one might wish to remain private receive prayers from all because of our God who sees and hears our prayers. Furthermore, members of the community who cannot be physically present on Sunday also know of the prayers for their concerns when they write those concerns on the cross.

As in the case of Link, the Prayer Pal Panda, we receive requests from others outside the community who see the cross in homes. In one circumstance, another of our Senior Evangelists asked for a cross for her neighbor. Her neighbor observed the cross with names and concerns written on it in this Evangelist's home and expressed her curiosity about the significance of the cross and the writings on it. After the neighbor learned how the Evangelist and the community use the cross, she asked to write her own prayer concerns on the cross. After some time of sharing the space on her cross, the Evangelist came to church and said, "I need a cross for my neighbor—she's using up too much of my space."

Wherever a person lives—independently at home, in assisted living, or more short-term in a hospital or even during a period of travel, the cross represents God's love lived out in this community of faith. The act of writing one's prayer concern or thanksgiving on the cross represents an act of faith. Erasing that writing may bring another prayer of thanksgiving for God's answer (in ways we may not yet understand) of those prayers.

A Cross to Wear

Almighty God, whose most dear Son went not up to joy but first he suffered pain, and entered not into glory before he was crucified: Mercifully grant that we, walking in the way of the cross, may find it none other than the way of life and peace; through Jesus Christ our Lord. Amen.

--Book of Common Prayer

Our Advent study began with discussion of our Baptismal promises. After our weeks of study and the beginning of our domestic church/monastic practices, we celebrated the Christmas season and then came once again to a time of reaffirmation of Baptismal vows as we celebrated the Baptism of Jesus in January.

On that day, each member of our congregation received a cross to wear—with distinctive blue ripples between the top cross and base to remind us of the waters of baptism.   Like some of the other outward and visible symbols we use, this cross became an item cherished by members of our faith community and often requested by others who see and inquire about this sign of our faith and community.

A JOURNEY JUST BEGUN. . .

A LITURGY OF CONTINUED BELONGING

See what love the Father has given us, that we should be called children of God; and that is what we are.

–I John 3:1 NRSV

As I planned and wrote this book, I took opportunities whenever I was among those in other congregations to ask some questions. One of those questions involved the percentage of people in a congregation over age 65; and the another asked how the congregation responds when one of the elders leaves. The answers (no surprise here) consistently provided the same information. Response to the first question: "Most of them". Response to the second, "If we know the person is leaving, we have a cake."

Until recently, responses from anyone in our congregation would be the same. However, we observed the need on the part of the departing person and in the continuing community to acknowledge the departure in a way which assured each other of our continued community of faith with our shared domestic church/monastic practices.

In our setting in a senior community, not only do people leave due to the loss of the ability to live independently, but every year some in our beloved seasonal community make the decision to give up the vacation home due to age, difficulty of travel, a medical diagnosis, or the increasing stresses from maintaining two homes.

We developed and use the liturgy "A Journey Just Begun". This liturgy reaffirms the continuation of our baptismal promises and our commitment to God and each other in our continued domestic church/monastic practices.

For one with a planned departure, we use the liturgy (always with the person's permission) on the Sunday prior to departure. If a person has had to move to assisted living, we follow the same process of first gaining permission from the individual and then inviting other members of the congregation to join the person for Holy Communion and this liturgy in the elder's new home. Always, of course, these plans change/adapt to individual situations and pastoral considerations. In all situations, the design of the liturgy gives the departing or recently moved elder the "presider" position and invites her/him to add/make changes in the prayers and music. When so many elements of this person's life now reflect loss and change, the community of faith provides this opportunity for the person to retain and exercise his/her leadership in the faith community.

Inviting friends and family from the community and in the new setting (i.e., assisted living) provides the opportunity for the elder to give witness, as a Senior Evangelist, to his/her faith in the larger community. In the assisted living setting, inviting those who work in the facility as well as other residents begins the elder's new/continued ministry as Evangelist in a new neighborhood.

In the latter setting, the faith community should be prepared to offer symbols and written materials of the domestic church/monasticism practices to others who may request them as a response to the elder's ministry among them. We pray for the work of the Senior Evangelist empowered by the Holy Spirit to lead others to domestic church/monastic practices.

The design for this Liturgy intends use after the sermon in the service of Holy Communion in the Sunday Service or in the person's new residential setting.

A JOURNEY JUST BEGUN. . .

Bless Us All

Life is full of sweet surprises, every day's a gift
The sun comes up and I can feel it lift my spirit
It fills me up with laughter, it fills me up with song
I look into the eyes of love and know that I belong.

Bless us all, who gather here
The loving family I hold dear
No place on Earth, compares with home
And every path will bring me back from where I roam.

Bless us all, that as we live
We always comfort and forgive
We have so much that we can share
With those in need we see around us everywhere.

Let us always love each other
Lead us toward the light
Let us hear the voice of reason
Singing in the night

Let us run from anger
And catch us when we fall
Teach us in our dreams and please, yes, please
Bless us one and all.

Bless us all with playful years
With noisy games and joyous tears
We reach for you, and we stand tall

And in our prayers and dreams we ask you bless us all
We reach for you, and we stand tall

And in our prayers and dreams we ask you bless us all.

N.: God of Wisdom, God of ageless love, you remain

faithful through every breath of our lives. (adapted,

Changes, Church Publishing Incorporated), p. 61)

Community: Give us grace to rejoice in your goodness

and hope and through your Spirit to continue our

journey with each other and in Christ, in whom we

gather and pray this day and always. (ibid)

N.: Loving Mother/Father God, bless our aging with

dignity and grace.

Community: Help us to accept who we are as we move from creation through earthly life to eternity. ("As Our Souls Move", A Prayer on Aging, https://reflections.yale.edu/article/test-time-art-aging/our-souls-move-prayer-aging)

N.: I ask the prayers and blessing of this community as I move to. . . .

Community: Our prayers and blessings go with you in this journey.

N.: I embark upon this part of my life and journey of

faith with the promise to continue, with God's help, in the apostle's teaching and fellowship, the breaking of the bread, and in prayers.

Community: With God's help, we hold you in this fellowship of love. We will pray for you in our daily prayers and as we meet at God's table.

N.: I take with me this shell as a reminder of my baptism, my life as a beloved child of God, and that I am marked as Christ's own forever.

Community: We give thanks for your life among us and for the gifts of the Holy Spirit in all our lives.

N.: I take Link with me as a symbol of our community of faith and our love and care for each other even when we cannot be physically together.

Community: Link goes with you as a sign of this community and of the faith and communion of God's Holy Church.

N.: I take with me these prayer beads as a symbol of our prayers for each other, our community, and for the world.

Community: May these prayer beads remind you that we pray together even when apart.

N.: I take this cross with me as a sign of Christ crucified; and, with God's help, I continue to proclaim His resurrection, and celebrate our eternal priesthood.

Community: Go in the power of the Holy Spirit to serve as God sustains you all the days of your life.

If N. desires, the community gathers around her/him for the following prayers and The Blessing.

N.: I give thanks to God, the Creator and sustainer of all life, for this and all my days. I am thankful for you, my community of faith, and thankful that I belong to the people of God. In these latter days of my earthly journey, I remain near to you and God, thankful for each day, and seeking the abundance of life to which God calls us.   I give God thanks and ask for God's help and your prayers and love. (adapted from Changes, p. 62)

Community: With thankful hearts, we commend you to God's love and care.   We pray for you and for ourselves that we may be young in hope and ageless in wisdom. As we continue the journey of our earthly lives, may we rejoice in the journey just begun in Jesus, the Resurrection and Life, who gives life for all time. Amen.   (adapted, ibid, p. 63)

The Blessing (adapted, ibid, p. 58)

N.: May our Mother/Father God hold us in love, every

day, for all time.

Community: May Christ, our Savior keep us in life, and
lead us to the joys of heaven.

N.: May the Holy Spirit, our companion on this journey
just begun, surround us and hold us in peace all our
days.   Amen.

She Comes Sailing on the Wind

Refrain:
She comes sailing on the wind,
her wings flashing in the sun;
on a journey just begun,
she flies on.
And in the passage of her flight,
her song rings out through the night,

full of laughter, full of light,
she flies on.

1. Silent waters rocking on the morning of our birth,
like an empty cradle waiting to be filled.
And from the heart of God the Spirit moved upon the
earth,
like a mother breathing life into her child.

2. Many were the dreamers whose eyes were given sight
when the Spirit filled their dreams with life and form.
Deserts turned to gardens, broken hearts found new
delight,
and then down the ages still she flew on.

(Refrain)

3. To a gentle girl in Galilee, a gentle breeze she came,
a whisper softly calling in the dark,
the promise of a child of peace whose reign would never
end,
Mary sang the Spirit song within her heart.

4. Flying to the river, she waited circling high
above the child now grown so full of grace.
As he rose up from the water, she swept down from the
sky,
and she carried him away in her embrace.

(Refrain)

5. Long after the deep darkness that fell upon the world,
after dawn returned in flame of rising sun,
the Spirit touched the earth again, again her wings
unfurled,
bringing life in wind and fire as she flew on.

(Refrain)

She Comes Sailing on the Wind, Gordon Light; <u>The Faith
We Sing</u>, No. 2122

The Service Continues with the Peace.

Preface For Holy Communion

From day to day, from age to age, throughout our lives in
this world and the next, you show yourself to be eternal
Love, giver and sustainer of all goodness and joy; and so
with all the saints of every generation who are ancient in
faith and young in hope, we join to sing your praise.
(<u>Changes</u>, p. 64)

Postscript

As our churches emptied and shelter-in-place orders demanded that each of us stay at home, many of our elders experienced intense isolation. While many churches provided online services of Morning and Evening Prayer, the elders in our local community of faith leaned more intensely into their domestic church/domestic church practices. The majority of our community members use little, if any, electronic devices beyond a basic cellular phone; so streaming videos of prayer and song did not reach them.

We had enjoyed two weeks of our Lenten Study (<u>Winged With Longing for Better Things</u> by Sylvia Sweeney), and the book with its assigned daily readings provided us with the connection of continued belonging as we each read the same readings and prayers each day. Those readings became even more important when suddenly we lived in a time of prohibited gatherings. We continued to read and pray together even while apart.

As the period of isolation extended into the Easter Season, I ordered each person a book which I had discovered during research for resources to support our community. Each person received <u>Common Prayer, A Liturgy for Ordinary Radicals</u>, (Zondervan Press), and each responded with joyful surprise and thankfulness after the postal service delivered the books to each home. Moving forward through these seemingly endless days stretching before us, we again had a common book of readings and prayers for use together while we were apart.

I chose this book from many for several reasons. The size, format, and font size work well for older hands and eyes. The book also becomes another outward and visible symbol of our community; and the layout of the book makes each day's reading easy to find and complete while also adding additional prayers and even some songs.

When we gather again, we will have much to share about this experience both as isolation and as community. Our community members share resources, and we will all surely bring our prayer and reading resources to share as we gather.

A great lesson from this time emphasizes the need to prepare in advance resources and materials ready to mail (including postage) if ever we find ourselves again in such a circumstance. Another lesson comes from the fact that we have now each experienced the reality of not being able to be physically present for community worship. We will have much to share for our own Spiritual Advanced Directive!

Some ideas for congregations which emerged (and each person and congregation will be able to build on these ideas and tailor them to individual and community needs) include:

- Providing *Forward Day by Day* booklets for members of the community
- Providing extra copies of those booklets to those who wish to share (as Senior Evangelists) to others who may include neighbors; roommates in hospital or care facilities; health aides
- Sending regular mailings (via postal service as well as electronic means) consisting of the Sunday Lectionary and Prayers of the People to those unable to attend services
- Asking those who cannot attend services to contribute to the Prayers of the People
- Using a congregational Cycle of Prayer in order for everyone—those present in church on Sunday and those unable to attend—to pray together for specific people and groups
- Developing and implementing a process for an Advanced Spiritual Directive

May the Holy Spirit inspire and guide us all through all our days as we love and serve God and each other in this life and in the life to come. Amen.

I will be your God throughout your lifetime—

Until your hair is white with age.

I made you, and I will care for you.

I will carry you along and save you.

—Isaiah 46:4 NRSV

End Notes

1. https://www.pewresearch.org/fact-tank/2016/07/11/which-u-s-religious-groups-are-oldest-and-youngest/

2. https://episcopalchurch.org/files/downloads/episcopal_congregations_overview_2014_1.pdf

3. https://www.prb.org/aging-unitedstates-fact-sheet/

4. Fredrica Harris Thompsett, Courageous Incarnation. (Cambridge, Massachusetts, 1993), p. 62.

5. Thornton Wilder, "The Long Christmas Dinner", Wilder's Classic One-Acts. (New York: Samuel French, 2012).

6. Naomi Levy, Einstein and the Rabbi. (New York: Flat Iron Books, 2017). Pp. 235-236.

7. https://www.prb.org/aging-unitedstates-fact-sheet/

8. Mitch Album, Tuesdays with Morrie. (New York: Broadway Books, 1997), p. 118.

9. Kathleen A. Chelan and Bonnie J. Miller-McLemore, eds., Calling All Years Good: Christian Vocation throughout Life's Seasons. (Grand Rapids, Michigan, 2017), p. 178.

10. Daniel B. Kaplan and Barbara J. Berkman, "Religion and Spirituality in the Elderly". https://www.merckmanuals.com/professional/geriatrics/social-issues-in-the-elderly/religion-and-spirituality-in-the-elderly.

11. Harold G. Koenig, <u>Aging and God</u>. (New York: The Haworth Pastoral Press, 1994), p. 294.

12. Diana Butler Bass, <u>Grounded</u>. (New York: Harper One, 2015), p. 134.

13. Ibid., P. 135.

14. David Jackson, et al. *"Spirituality, spiritual need, and spiritual care in aged care: What the literature says"*, Journal of Religion, Spirituality, and Aging. https://www.tandfonline.com/doi/abs/10.1080/15528030.2016.1193097?journalCode=wrsa20.

15. Joan Chittister, <u>The Gift of Years: Growing Older Gracefully</u>. (New York: BlueBridge, 2008), p. 103.

16. Ibid., p. 103.

17. Daniel B. Kaplan and Barbara J. Berkman. "Religion and Spirituality in the Elderly". https://www.merckmanuals.com/professional/geriatrics/social-issues-in-the-elderly/religion-and-spirituality-in-the-elderly.

18. Andrew J. Weaver, Harold G. Koenig, and Phyllis C. Roe, <u>Reflections on Aging and Spiritual Growth</u>. (Nashville: Abingdon Press, 1998), p. 34.

19. Elizabeth MacKinlay, et al. "Aging, Spirituality and Pastoral Care: A Multi-National Perspective", 2001 *Journal of Religious Gerontology*, Volume 12, Numbers 3 & 4.

20. Anonymous. "Seniors and Spirituality: Health Benefits of Faith". Elder Care Alliance. <u>https://eldercarealliance.org/blog/seniors-and-spirituality-health-benefits-of-faith</u>.

21. Manning, Lydia K. "Spirituality as a Lived Experience: Exploring the Essence of Spirituality for Women in Late Life", 75 (2), 2012 *International Journal of Aging and Human Development*. 2012: 75 (2). <u>https://www.ncbi.nlm.nih.gov/pmc/articles/PMC3572539</u>.

22. Harold G. Koenig, <u>Aging and God</u>. (New York: The Haworth Pastoral Press, 1994),126.

23. <u>Book of Common Prayer</u>, "Burial Rite I", (New York: Church Publishing Incorporated, 1986), p. 488.

24. R. Paul Stevens, <u>Aging Matters: Finding Your Calling for the Rest of Your Life</u>. (Grand Rapids, Michigan: William B. Eerdmans Publishing Company, 2016), p. 72.

25. Holly Nelson-Becker and Kimberly Sangster. "Recapturing the power of ritual to enhance community in aging", *Journal of Religion, Spirituality & Aging.* 01 November, 2018. https://www.researchgate.net/publication/328683678_Recapturing_the_power_of_ritual_to_enhance_community_in_aging.

26. David Jackson, et al. *"Spirituality, spiritual need, and spiritual care in aged care: What the literature says"*, Journal of Religion, Spirituality, and Aging. https://www.tandfonline.com/doi/abs/10.1080/15528030.2016.1193097?journalCode=wrsa20.

27. Mitch Album, Tuesdays with Morrie. (New York: Broadway Books, 1997), p. 118.

28. Harold G. Koenig, Aging and God. (New York: The Haworth Pastoral Press, 1994), Pp. 127-128

29. William M. Clements, ed., Ministry with the Aging: Designs, Challenges, Foundations. (New York: The Haworth Press, 1989), p. 162.

30. Kathleen A. Cahalan and Bonnie J. Miller-McLemore, eds., Calling All Years Good: Christian Vocation throughout Life's Seasons. (Grand Rapids, Michigan, 2017), p. 194.

31. Ibid., p. 177.

32. Ibid., p. 178

33. Elizabeth MacKinlay. <u>The Spiritual Dimension of Ageing</u>. (London: Jessica Kingsley Publishers, 2001), p. 153.

34. Harold G. Koenig. <u>Purpose and Power in Retirement</u>. (Philadelphia: Templeton Foundation Press, 2002), Pp. 114-115.

35. Parker Palmer. <u>On the Brink of Everything: Grace, Gravity, and Getting Old</u>. (San Francisco: Berrett-Koehler Publishers, 2018), p. 145.

36. Ibid., p. 159.

37. Harold G. Koenig. <u>Purpose and Power in Retirement</u>. (Philadelphia: Templeton Foundation Press, 2002), p. 121.

38. Rami M. Shapiro. <u>Minyan</u>. (New York: Bell Tower, 1997), p. 100.

39. Kathleen A. Cahalan and Bonnie J. Miller-McLemore, eds., <u>Calling All Years Good: Christian Vocation throughout Life's Seasons.</u> (Grand Rapids, Michigan, 2017), p. 185.

40. Thomas P. Rausch. <u>Radical Christian Communities</u>. (Eugene, Oregon: Wipf and Stock Publishers, 1990), p. 16.

41. Kathleen A. Cahalan and Bonnie J. Miller-McLemore, eds., <u>Calling All Years Good: Christian</u>

Vocation throughout Life's Seasons. (Grand Rapids, Michigan, 2017), p. 185.

42. Holly Nelson-Becker and Kimberly Sangster. "Recapturing the power of ritual to enhance community in aging", *Journal of Religion, Spirituality & Aging.* 01 November, 2018. https://www.researchgate.net/publication/328683678_ Recapturing_the_power_of_ritual_to_enhance_commu nity_in_aging.

43. Holly Nelson-Becker and Kimberly Sangster. "Recapturing the power of ritual to enhance community in aging", *Journal of Religion, Spirituality & Aging.* 01 November, 2018. https://www.researchgate.net/publication/328683678_ Recapturing_the_power_of_ritual_to_enhance_commu nity_in_aging.

44. David Jackson, et al. *"Spirituality, spiritual need, and spiritual care in aged care: What the literature says"*, Journal of Religion, Spirituality, and Aging. https://www.tandfonline.com/doi/abs/10.1080/155280 30.2016.1193097?journalCode=wrsa20.

45. Elizabeth MacKinlay, et al. "Aging, Spirituality and Pastoral Care: A Multi-National Perspective", 2001 *Journal of Religious Gerontology*, Volume 12, Numbers 3 & 4.

46. Harold G. Koenig, <u>Aging and God</u>. (New York: The Haworth Pastoral Press, 1994), 127-128.

47. Pew Research Center. "Spirituality and Aging: A Guide for Seniors on Faith, Meaning, and Connection", Religious Landscape Study. <u>https://www.greatseniorliving.com/articles/spirituality</u>.

48. David O. Moberg, <u>Aging and Spirituality</u>. Oxfordshire, United Kingdom: Routledge, 2001, 134.

49. Joan Chittister, <u>The Gift of Years: Growing Older Gracefully</u>. (New York: BlueBridge, 2008), 103.

50. Dwight W. Vogel, ed., <u>Primary Sources of Liturgical Theology</u>. (Collegeville, Minnesota: Liturgical Press, 2001), p. 274.

51. Ibid., p. 275.

52. http://www.catholiccincinnati.org/ministries-offices/family-life/family/parenting/what-is-a-domestic-church/

53. http://www.usccb.org/beliefs-and-teachings/vocations/parents/tools-for-building-a-domestic-church.cfm

54. Ibid.

55. Thomas Knieps, Port Le Roi, Gerard Mannion, and Peter De Mey. <u>The Household of God and Local</u>

Households: Revisiting the Domestic Church. (Paris: Peeters, 2013), p. 181.

56. Ibid., p. 186.

57. Ibid., p. 191.

58. Ibid., p. 179.

59. Ibid., p. 180.

60. Elizabeth Rapley. The Lord as Their Portion: The Story of the Religious Orders and How They Changed Our World. (Grand Rapids, Michigan: William B. Eerdmans Publishing Company, 2011), p. x.

61.Christopher Jamison. Finding Happiness: Monastic Steps for a Fulfilling Life. (Collegeville, Minnesota: Liturgical Press, 2008), p. 2.

62. Ibid., p. 2.

63. Manning, Lydia K. "Spirituality as a Lived Experience: Exploring the Essence of Spirituality for Women in Late Life", 75 (2) 2012*International Journal of Aging and Human Development*. 2012: 75 (2). (https://www.ncbi.nlm.nih.gov/pmc/articles/PMC3572 539.

64. Christopher Jamison. Finding Happiness: Monastic Steps for a Fulfilling Life. (Collegeville, Minnesota: Liturgical Press, 2008), p. 57.

65. Paul Wilkes. Beyond the Walls: Monastic Wisdom for Everyday Life. (Chicago: ACTA Publications, 2010), p. 68.

66. Dirk G. Lange and Dwight W. Vogel. ORDO: Bath, Word, Prayer, Table. (Claremont, California: OSL Publications, 2018), 57.

67. David O. Moberg, Aging and Spirituality. Oxfordshire, United Kingdom: Routledge, 2001, 134.

68. Paul Wilkes. Beyond the Walls: Monastic Wisdom for Everyday Life. (Chicago: ACTA Publications, 2010), p. 235.

69. Greg Peters, The Monkhood of All Believers: The Monastic Foundation of Christian Spirituality. (Grand Rapids, Michigan: Baker Academic, 2018), p. 66.

70. Paul Wilkes. Beyond the Walls: Monastic Wisdom for Everyday Life. (Chicago: ACTA Publications, 2010), p. 231.

71. Andrea Sherman, "Interview: The Power of Ritual to Transform Lives", *Aging Horizons Bulletin*. https://aginghorizons.com/2009/05/interview-the-power-of-ritual-to-transform-lives.

72. Ibid.

73. Dwight W. Vogel, ed., Primary Sources of Liturgical Theology. (Collegeville, Minnesota: Liturgical Press, 200), 291.

74. J.E. Dearlove, "J.B.: The Artistry of Ambiguity", *The Christian Century*, 19 May, 1976. https://www.religion-online.org/article/j-b-the-artistry-of-ambiguity.

75. Ibid.

76. Ibid.

77. Julia Gatta. Life in Christ: Practicing Christian Spirituality. (New York: Church Publishing Incorporated, 2018), p. 129.

Sources and Resources

Abraham, John. How to Get the Death You Want. Hinesbury, Vermont: Upper Access Books, 2017.

Album, Mitch. Tuesdays with Morrie. New York: Broadway Books, 1997.

Anderson, Herbert and Edward Foley. Mighty Stories, Dangerous Rituals. San Francisco: Jossey-Bass Publishers, 1998.

Anonymous. The Cloud of Unknowing. Kindle. (no publication information).

Anonymous. "Seniors and Spirituality: Health Benefits of Faith". Elder Care Alliance. https://eldercarealliance.org/blog/seniors-and-spirituality-health-benefits-of-faith.

Bass, Diana Butler. Grounded. New York: Harper One, 2015.

Becker, Arthur H. Ministry with Older Persons. Minneapolis: Augsburg Publishing House, 1986.

Book of Common Prayer. (New York: Church Publishing Incorporated, 1986).

Bone, Alison. "Why rituals are still important.", https://www.sbs.com.au/topics/life/culture/article/2016/06/27/why-rituals-are-still-relevant

Breidenthal, Thomas E. <u>Christian Households</u>. Eugene, Oregon: Wipf & Stock, 1989.

Cahalan, Kathleen A. and Bonnie J. Miller-McLemore. <u>Calling All Years Good</u>. Grand Rapids, Michigan: William B. Eerdmans Publishing Company, 2017.

Chittister, Joan. <u>The Gift of Years: Growing Older Gracefully</u>. New York: BlueBridge, 2008.

Clements, William M. <u>Ministry with the Aging: Designs, Challenges, Foundations</u>. New York: The Haworth Press, 1989.

Dearlove, J.E. "J.B.: The Artistry of Ambiguity", *The Christian Century*, 19 May, 1976. https://www.religion-online.org/article/j-b-the-artistry-of-ambiguity.

Diocese of Oxford. "Believing without Belonging." Oxford: SCOP, 2008. <u>https://www.oxford.anglican.org/archive/SCOP/Believing without Belonging.pdf.</u>

Diocese of Oxford. "A Theology of Ageing; Ageing Well". Oxford: SCOP, 2008. <u>https://www.oxford.anglican.org/archive/SCOP/Theology of Ageing.pdf</u>.

Diocese of Oxford. "Worship with Older People." Oxford, SCOP, 2008. https://www.oxford.anglican.org/archive/SCOP/Worship with Older People.pdf.

Erichsen, Nora-Beata and Arndt Bussing. "Spiritual Needs of Elderly Living in Residential/Nursing Homes", *Hindawi: Evidence-Based Complementary and Alternative Medicine*, Volume 2013, Article ID 913247. https://www.hindawi.com/ journals/ecam/2013/913247/

Fracchia, Charles A. Living Together Alone. San Francisco: Harper & Row, 1979.

Gatta, Julia. Life in Christ: Practicing Christian Spirituality. New York: Church Publishing Incorporated, 2018.

Garfield, Charles. Life's Last Gift. Last Vegas: Central Recovery Press, 2017.

Gordon, Nancy and Richard Address. "Rituals as Markers of Transition", 7th International Conference on Ageing and Spirituality, 9 January, 2017. https://www.7thinternationalconference.org/single-post/2017/01/09/Rituals-as-Markers-of-Transition.

Grudzen, Marita. "Rituals as portals of transcendence in the lives of older adults." Journal of Religion, Spirituality, and Aging. Volume 30, 2018, Issue 2.

https://www.tandfonline.com/doi/abs/10.1080/155280
30.2017.1312725

Hampton, Roy and Charles Russell. "Ideas about
Aging in Literature," *MedRounds*.
http://www.medrounds.org/encyclopedia-of-
aging/2006/01/ideas-about-aging-in-literature.html.

Hays, Edward. Prayers for a Planetary Pilgrim. Notre
Dame: Forest of Peace, 2008.

Henes, Mama Donna. "Why We Need Rituals in Our
Lives", *Huffington Post: LIFE, the Blog*. 17 July,
2013.
https://www.huffpost.com/entry/rituals_n_3294412.

Imber-Black, Evan and Janine Roberts. Rituals for
Our Times. Northvale, New Jersey: Jason Aronson,
Inc., 1998.

Jackson, David, et al. *"Spirituality, spiritual need, and
spiritual care in aged care: What the literature says"*,
Journal of Religion, Spirituality, and Aging.
https://www.tandfonline.com/doi/abs/10.1080/155280
30.2016.1193097?journalCode=wrsa20.

Jamison, Abbot Christopher, Finding Happiness:
Monastic Steps for a Fulfilling Life. Collegeville,
Minnesota: Liturgical Press, 2008.

Jones, Cheslyn, Geoffrey Wainwright, Edward Yarnold, SJ, and Paul Bradshaw, eds. The Study of Liturgy. London: Oxford University Press, 1992.

Kaplan, Daniel B. and Barbara J. Berkman. "Religion and Spirituality in the Elderly". https://www.merckmanuals.com/professional/geriatrics /social-issues-in-the-elderly/religion-and-spirituality-in-the-elderly.

Kimble, Melvin A., Susan H. McFadden, James W. Eliot, and James J. Seeber, eds. Aging, Spirituality, and Religion, Volume I. Minneapolis: Fortress Press, 1995.

Klaushofer, Alex. The New Monastics. Kindle, 2016.

Koenig, Harold G. "Integrating Spirituality into the Care of Older Adults," Cambridge Core. https://www.cambridge.org/core/journals/international-psychogeriatrics/article/integrating-spirituality-into-the-care-of-older-adults/C9058DEA95C1AEDF4C18579C38DCF9B7.

Koenig, Harold G. Aging and God. New York: The Haworth Pastoral Press, 1994.

Koenig, Harold G. Purpose and Power in Retirement. Philadelphia: Templeton Foundation Press, 2003.

Kubler-Ross, Elisabeth. The Wheel of Life. New York: Simon & Schuster, 1997.

Knieps, Thomas, Port Le Roi, Gerard Mannion, Peter De Mey. The Households of God and Local Households. Paris: Peeters,, 2013.

Knox, Ian S. Older People and the Church. London: T&T Clark, 2005.

Lange, Dirk G. and Dwight W. Vogel. ORDO: Bath, Word, Prayer, Table. Claremont, California: OSL Publications, 2018.

Lathrop, Gordon W. Holy Ground. Minneapolis: Fortress Press, 2009.

Levy, Naomi. Einstein and the Rabbi. New York: Flat Iron Books, 2017.

MacKinlay, Elizabeth. The Spiritual Dimension of Ageing. London and Philadelphia: Jessica Kingsley Publishers, 2001.

MacKinlay, Elizabeth, James W. Ellor, and Stephen Pickard, eds. "Aging, Spirituality and Pastoral Care: A Multi-National Perspective". *Journal of Religious Gerontology*, Volume 12, Numbers 3 and 4, 2001.

MacLeish, Archibald. J.B., New York: Houghton-Mifflin, 1956.

Manning, Lydia K. "Spirituality as a Lived Experience: Exploring the Essence of Spirituality for Women in Late Life", : 75 (2) 2012*International Journal of Aging and Human Development*. 2012: 75 (2). https://www.ncbi.nlm.nih.gov/pmc/articles/PMC3572539.

Moberg, David O. Aging and Spirituality. Oxfordshire, United Kingdom: Routledge, 2001.

Mowat, Harriett and Maureen O'Neill. "Insights: Spirituality and Aging". https://www.iriss.org.uk/resources/insights/spirituality-ageing-implications-care-support-older-people.

Nelson-Becker, Holly and Kimberly Sangster. "Recapturing the power of ritual to enhance community in aging", *Journal of Religion, Spirituality & Aging*. 01 November, 2018. https://www.researchgate.net/publication/328683678_Recapturing_the_power_of_ritual_to_enhance_community_in_aging.

O'Murchu. Adult Faith. Maryknoll, New York: Orbis Books, 2011.

Palmer, Parker. On the Brink of Everything. Berrett-Koelher Publishers, Inc., 2018

Peek, Marike. "The Importance of Ritual and Ceremony", *Network Ireland*, 12 June, 2015.

https://networkmagazine.ie/articles/importance-ritual-and-ceremony.

Peters, Greg. The Monkhood of All Believers. Grand Rapids, Michigan: Baker Academic, 2018.

Pew Research Center. "Spirituality and Aging: A Guide for Seniors on Faith, Meaning, and Connection", Religious Landscape Study. https://www.greatseniorliving.com/articles/spirituality.

Plass, Mark. The Inner Room: A Journey into Lay Monasticism. Cincinnati: St. Anthony Messenger Press, 2000.

Population Reference Bureau, 2019.

Ramshaw, Gail. Pray, Praise, and Give Thanks: A Collection of Litanies. Laments, and Thanksgivings at Font and Table. Minneapolis: Augsburg Press, 2017.

Ramshaw, Elaine. Ritual and Pastoral Care. Philadelphia: Fortress Press, 1987.

Rapley, Elizabeth. The Lord as Their Portion. Grand Rapids: William B. Eerdmans Publishing Company, 2011.

Rausch, Thomas P., S.J. Radical Christian Communities. Eugene, Oregon: Wipf and Stock Publishers, 1990.

Rees, Daniel and Other Members of the English Benedictine Congregation. <u>Consider Your Call: A Theology of Monastic Life Today</u>. London: SPCK, 1978.

Rochat, Etiene, et al. "A Resource for Interprofessional Providers: Spiritual Needs of Hospitalized Older Adults", *Elder Care*. Arizona State University, Arizona Center on Aging, May, 2015. <u>https://nursingandhealth.asu.edu/sites/default/files/spiritual-needs-of-hospitalized-older-adults.pdf</u>.

Rolheiser, Ronald. <u>Domestic Monastery</u>. Brewster, Massachusetts: Paraclete Press, 2019.

Sherman, Andrea. "Interview: The Power of Ritual to Transform Lives", *Aging Horizons Bulletin*. <u>https://aginghorizons.com/2009/05/interview-the-power-of-ritual-to-transform-lives</u>.

Shapiro, Rami M. <u>Minyan</u>. New York: Bell Tower, 1997.

Simmons, Henry C. and Jane Wilson. <u>Soulful Aging</u>. Smyth & Helwys Publishing, Inc., 2001.

Standing Commission on Liturgy and Music of the Episcopal Church. <u>Changes</u>. New York: Church Publishing Incorporated, 2007.

Stevens, R. Paul. _Aging Matters_. Grand Rapids, Michigan: William B. Eerdmans Publishing Company, 2016.

Stillman, William. "Why are rituals important to spirituality?", https://www.sharecare.com/health/spiritual-wellness-religion/rituals-and-spirituality.

Swenson, Harriet Kerr. _Visible and Vital_. New York: Paulist Press, 1994.

Terranova, Jacob. "What Are Rituals, and Why Do We Need Them?", https://www.frazerconsultants.com/2016/07/what-are-rituals-and-why-do-we-need-them.

Thompsett, Fredrica Harris. _Courageous Incarnation_. Cambridge, Massachusetts: Cowley Publications, 1993.

Thompson, Sylvia. "New Monasticism movement: a modern take on an old tradition", _Irish Times_. 13 February, 2013. https://www.irishtimes.com/life-and-style/people/new-monasticism-movement-a-modern-take-on-an-old-tradition-1.1251809.

Tillberg, Cedric, ed. _The Fullness of Life_. Lutheran Church in America: Division for Mission in North America, 1980.

Vogel, Dwight W., ed. <u>Primary Sources of Liturgical Theology</u>. Collegeville, Minnesota: Liturgical Press, 2001.

Vogel, Dwight W. and Linda J. Vogel. <u>Sacramental Living</u>. Nashville: Upper Room Books, 1999.

Wattis, John and Stephen Curran. "How Spirituality Can Help Us Cope with the Trails of Ageing," *The Conversation*. <u>http://theconversation.com/how-spirituality-can-help-us-cope-with-the-trials-of-ageing-58180</u>.

Weaver, Andrew J., Harold G. Koenig, and Phyllis C. Roe, eds. <u>Reflections on Aging and Spiritual Growth</u>. Nashville: Abingdon Press, 1998.

Wilder, Thornton. "The Long Christmas Dinner", <u>Wilder's Classic One-Acts</u>. New York: Samuel French, 2012.

Wilkes, Paul. <u>Beyond the Walls: Monastic Wisdom for Everyday Life</u>. New York: Doubleday, 1999.

Youngblood, Desiree M. "Purpose in Practices: Spiritual Landscapes of Older Adults," *The Presbyterian Outlook*, 2017. <u>https://pres-outlook.org/2017/01/purpose-in-practices-spiritual-landscapes-of-older-adults</u>.